The Prophets

Syed Ali Ashraf

Ta-Ha Publishers Ltd.
1 Wynne Road
London
SW9 0BB

Published in Muharram 1417/May 1996 by
Ta-Ha Publishers Ltd, 1 Wynne Road, London SW9 0BB

British Library Cataloguing in Publication Data: A catalogue record for this book is available from the British Library.

ISBN 1 897940 40 8

Artwork: Design and illustrations by Meena Jamil and M. Ishaq.
Qur'anic verses in Kufic script by Bayoumi.

Printed and Bound in Great Britain by Deluxe Printers, London.

Meanings of Qur'anic verses written in Arabic Calligraphy

Front Cover: In the Name of Allah, the Most Gracious, the Most Merciful. Say: 'He is Allah, the One and Only; Allah, the Eternal, Absolute; He begets not, nor is He begotten; and there is none like Him.' (*Qur'an: 112*)

Back Cover: We make no distinction between any of His Prophets. (*Qur'an: 2.285*)

Chapter 1: To Him is due the primal origin of the heavens and the earth: when He decrees a matter, He says to it: 'Be' and it is. (*Qur'an: 2.117*)

Chapter 2: I will create a viceregent on earth. (*Qur'an: 2.30*)

Chapter 3: We sent Noah to his people with the command: 'Warn your people before there comes to them a grievous punishment. (*Qur'an: 71.1*)

Chapter 4: I will make you a model leader for mankind. (*Qur'an: 2.124*)

Chapter 5: 'O my Lord: You have indeed bestowed on me some power, and have taught me something of the interpretation of dreams and events.' (*Qur'an: 12.101*)

Chapter 6: 'O Moses, I have chosen you above other men, by the mission I have given you and by the words I have spoken to you.' (*Qur'an: 7.144*)

Chapter 7: 'O David, We did indeed make you a viceregent on earth.' (*Qur'an: 38.26*)

Chapter 8: To David We gave Solomon for a son – how excellent in Our service. Ever did he turn to Us. (*Qur'an: 38.30*)

Chapter 9: The similitude of Jesus before Allah is as that of Adam. (*Qur'an: 3.59*)

Chapter 10: We have not sent you except as a mercy to all the worlds. (*Qur'an: 21.107*)

Thanksgiving

In the Name of Allah, the Beneficent, the Merciful

Praise be to Allah, the Lord of the Worlds, and peace and blessings of Allah be upon Prophet Muhammad, the Most Eminent of Messengers.

I offer my thanks first and foremost to Allah who helped me in writing this book. Peace and blessings of Allah be on Prophet Muhammad without whose recorded sayings and doings it would have been impossible to explain most of the incidents related in this book. Peace and blessings of Allah be on all other Prophets whose lives have provided me with inspiration.

Next, my thanks are due to friends and relations who read the manuscript and offered valuable suggestions. I am deeply indebted to Professor Muhammad Qutb for having gone through the book with me line by line, suggesting alterations and modifications so that there would be no deviation from the orthodox Islamic viewpoint. I am grateful to my cousin Professor Sajjad Hussain and my colleague at King Abdulaziz University, Jeddah, Mr. G. W. Groos, who looked at words, phrases and concepts from the point of view of their suitability, and made useful suggestions and comments. I thank also Meena Jamil for the sincerity and love with which she used her artistic skill in order to convey meaning through pictures.

May Allah keep all my friends and relations on the right path.

Cambridge
England

Syed Ali Ashraf

A Letter To Muslim Parents and Teachers

Dear Parents and Teachers,

This book has been written for your children so that they may know something about our great prophets. It is for you to read these life stories to them when they are very young and like to listen to stories before they go to bed. It is for you also to answer any question that these children might ask. Children who are nine or ten years of age will probably be able to read these stories themselves. But they may still have questions whose answers they may not find here. I would therefore request you to help your children so that they may grow up with an Islamic attitude towards the past.

As you all know, Islam declares that Allah is *One*, there is *One* human race and there has always been *One* religion. It also claims that the first man was made by Allah and he was taught this religion so that he might teach his children how to stay on the right path. But man strayed from this path from time to time. That was when Allah chose certain individuals and called them his Prophets who tried their best to keep men and women on the right path. We Muslims believe that of these Prophets the last and most eminent was Prophet Muhammad, peace and blessings of Allah be on him.

In this book we have told the life-history of nine well-known Prophets, up to the Prophet Muhammad, may the blessings and peace of Allah be on them. Allah says in the Qurar that He has chosen Prophets from other races and tribes in other places of the world, but as the Quran does not describe them, we cannot be sure who they were. That is why we have ignored them.

We have retained the original Arabic names of the Prophets so that Muslim children may use these names in their traditional form as given in the Quran. We would request you, dear parents and teachers, to tell Muslim children to use these Quranic names and not the English versions given in the Bible. They will then be more conscious of their own cultural heritage. The *dua* or prayer recited after the names of the Prophets − "peace be on him" − is to be learnt and practised by students because this is a good practice that Prophet Muhammad, peace and blessings of Allah be on him, has asked us to keep up. Thus Muslim children will be able to demonstrate to non-Muslim children how they show respect to all Prophets. For the history of these Prophets, we have relied only on the Quran and the Hadith. And of the six authentic collections of Hadith we depended mainly on *Bukhari* and *Muslim*. Our version is the Muslim version of their stories and that is why this version differs from the Biblical version. It is not necessary for you to discuss this difference because children should know only what we believe in. They are too young to discuss differences.

I have tried to relate the stories in as simple a language as possible and I hope your children, and you also, will enjoy them.

Syed Ali Ashraf

iv

Contents

Illustrations

بديع السموات والأرض واذا قضى أمراً فانما يقول له كن فيكون

Before Man In The Beginning

Allah is all-powerful. He is the maker of everything – the Sun, the Moon, the Sky, the Seas, the Hills, the Trees. When He wants to make anything He says "Be" and it is made.

In the beginning there was only God. There was no Sun, no Sky, no Moon, no Earth, no Man, no animals, no birds.

Then Allah wanted them and they came to life.

Creation of Angels

He made angels to serve Him. They are made out of light. They do not die. They can go anywhere Allah wants them to go. They can do anything Allah wants them to do. Allah has distributed work among them. Some angels are superior to others. They are known as archangels. Jibreel (peace be on him) is one of them. He is the angel of life. He is also a messenger. He brings Allah's message to messengers on Earth who are human beings. Azrail (peace be on him) is another archangel. He is the messenger of death. He takes away our souls when Allah wants us to leave the earth. There are millions and millions of angels, each doing his job.

The Sky, Suns, Moons, Stars and Worlds

He made the sky. He wanted the Sun, the Moon, the Stars, the Planets to be made. They all were made. Then He placed them in the sky. He ordered them to move. But He has made laws for them. They all follow a rule. That is why they do not hit each other. If they do, they will get broken. Nothing will remain.

Allah Made the Animals

Allah also made animals. He placed them on this earth. We do not know how many kinds of animals or birds there were. Long, long ago there were large animals. Some of them, which we call dinosaurs, were very large. We have found some skeletons of dinosaurs. They died many, many years ago.

Allah made other animals. Some of them, the monkeys and the apes, were like men. Even gorillas looked like gigantic men.

Jinns

Allah made the jinns. They were made of fire. They could take any shape they liked. They could become invisible. They knew some way of getting through locked doors which we do not know. But they gradually started misbehaving. They would not pray or have faith. Then Allah punished them. But a child, Iblis, was taken to Heaven. He grew up with the angels. He prayed with them and lived with them in Heaven.

Though Allah punished the jinns, He did not kill all of them. Those jinns who are living on the earth now are great-great-great-grandchildren of those who were living at that time. The good jinns believe in Allah, pray to Him and do good deeds. But we cannot see them with the naked eye unless they take some shape or form.

We make no distinction between
one and another of His Prophets

Adam
(peace be on him)

The Creation of Adam

Allah decided to give mastery of the Earth and the entire creation to Man. He then made the first Man out of clay. Three other things — fire, air and water — were also used to make this new creature. From His own spirit Allah breathed into the new creature. It woke up as if it had been asleep. This first Man was Adam (peace be on him).

Adam (peace be on him) and the Angels

Allah then taught Adam (peace be on him) the meaning of everything. He knew what the sky was for, what the stars were doing, why the Sun, the Moon, the planets were created. He knew why Allah wanted to make everything.

Allah then called the angels. He asked them the meaning of everything. As Allah had not taught them the meaning they could not tell Him. They bowed to Allah and said, "O Allah, we can tell you only what you have taught us."

Allah then asked Adam (peace be on him) to tell them the meaning. He told them.

Allah then told the angels "Bow down and show respect to Adam."

All of them bowed down except Iblis.

Allah asked him, "Why have you not obeyed My order?"

He said, "O Allah, You made me out of fire and You made Adam out of clay. I am better than he is."

Satan Decides to Mislead Adam (peace be on him)

Iblis was proud. He disobeyed Allah. He therefore tried to show that he could disobey, that he had authority. This was wrong. Allah was his Creator and Master. All power comes from Allah. It was foolish of Iblis to think that he had power. Allah therefore cursed him. He said, "You are cursed, you are Satan."

Iblis whose name became Satan, prayed to Allah, "O Allah, give me power to lead this Adam and his children away from Your path. Give me power to enter into his body and mind and make him do bad things and think wrong things. As I am going to suffer for this man, O Allah, give me power to show how weak this creature is."

Allah said, "You will not be able to do any harm to a person who will follow My orders and live a good life. You will not be able to mislead him."

This means that Satan can mislead only those who disobey Allah's orders, because then they also behave like Satan.

How Satan Cheated Adam and Eve (peace be on them)

Adam (peace be on him) was at first alone. He felt lonely. Allah took a rib out of him and created a woman. Adam gave her the name Hawa (Eve) (peace be on her). They loved each other and were happy. Allah then said to Adam, "Stay here. Eat whatever you like. But do not go near that tree. If you do so you will come to harm, and you will suffer."

Satan had now become Adam's deadly enemy. He heard what Allah told him. He therefore planned to mislead Adam (peace be on him). Allah had warned Adam (peace be on him), "Iblis is your enemy. Do not trust him. He will mislead you."

Adam (peace be on him) forgot this warning. Satan took the form of a serpent and whispered to him, "Shall I tell you how you can become like the angels, how you can live for ever?"

"How?"

"Eat the fruit of that tree. You will then know how you can be immortal."

Adam and Hawa (peace be on them) forgot Allah's warning and ate from that tree. Immediately they lost their heavenly dress and became naked. They took leaves from trees and sewed them together in order to cover their shame.

The Fall of Adam (peace be on him)

Allah told Adam and Hawa (peace be on them), "That serpent is Satan. From now on you are going to be enemies. And from now on you will all have to live on Earth for a short period, die and come back to me."

Adam and Hawa (peace be on them) started weeping and praying. They knew they had disobeyed Allah. They prayed to Allah to forgive them.

Allah sent them down to this Earth.

He said, "Your sons and daughters and their children will live on the Earth. They will all die and come back to Me. But many of them will forget my teaching and all the things that I have taught you. So from time to time I shall send my learning to some good men. They will be My Prophets. They will call men to the right path. Those who will not follow them will be punished in Hell. I shall send such men to all those parts of the world where your children will live."

Adam (peace be on him) Comes to Arafat

But their sufferings were not over. Adam (peace be on him) was sent to Mount Budh (in Ceylon) and Hawa (peace be on her) was sent to the Red Sea coast. Allah told Adam (peace be on him) to go to Bakka valley. Bakka was the early name of present Mecca. After travelling to various places Adam (peace be on him) saw the valley of Mecca where he found a throne that Allah had sent. He built a stone house round about it and called it Kaa'ba. After this he went to Arafat and stood on a hill and prayed to Allah for forgiveness. Hawa (peace be on her) also had reached that place. They again met. That hill is still called Jabal-i-Rahmah — the Hill of Mercy — because Allah forgave them both when Adam and Hawa (peace be on them) wept and prayed for forgiveness just before sunset. That is why Muslims go to Arafat on the 9th day of the lunar month Zilhajj and pray to Allah before sunset.

Habil and Qabil

For many years Adam and Hawa (peace be on them) lived on this Earth. They had two sets of twins — each a boy and a girl. The boy of the first twins would marry the girl of the second twins. So also the girl of the first twins would marry the boy of the second twins.

Qabil was from the first set of twins and Habil was from the second set.

Qabil was the elder boy and Habil the younger. Habil was very good but Qabil was not. Habil was liked by everyone. Qabil was jealous.

One day both of them sacrificed an animal to God. Allah's fire came and burnt Habil's sacrifice.

Qabil became angry, and full of jealousy. He said to Habil, "I shall kill you."

Habil said, "There must be something wrong with you. You pray to Allah and ask Allah to forgive you. Why should you kill me? I am not going to kill you even if you strike me. Allah sees everything. If you kill me you will be sorry. Allah will punish you and send you to Hell."

Qabil got angry. He did not want to hear anything from Habil. He hated him. So he struck him with a stone and killed him.

This was the first time a man had killed a man.

Qabil saw the dead body. He did not know what to do.

Allah sent two angels in the shape of big crows. One of them seemed to kill the other. Then the killer dug a grave in the sand with his beak and claws, put the other crow in it and put sand on it. Then it flew away.

So Qabil learnt what to do. He dug a grave for his brother and put him inside the grave.

Allah cursed him. Qabil became very; very sorry for what he had done. All his life he roamed. He moved from place to place but he could never be happy, he could never rest, he could never sleep.

إِنَّا أَرْسَلْنَا نُوحًا إِلَىٰ قَوْمِهِ أَنْ أَنْذِرْ قَوْمَكَ مِنْ قَبْلِ أَنْ يَأْتِيَهُمْ عَذَابٌ أَلِيمٌ

Nooh
(peace be on him)

Before the Flood

Many, many years passed. Adam's family increased. Adam and Hawa (peace be on them) died and went back to Heaven. There were many men and women in different places. But they often forgot Adam's teachings. Allah had to send Prophets to teach them what they should do and what they should not do.

A time came when men became proud like Satan and would not listen to the Prophets. Allah sent Nooh (peace be on him) to them. By this time these people had made their own gods and goddesses. They had a Man-god called *Wadd* and a Woman-goddess called *Suwa*. For strength they would go to their lion-god called *Yaguth*. For power to ride and fight they would pray to their horse-god *Ya-uq*. And for all other kinds of help they would pray to their eagle-god *Nasr*.

Nooh (peace be on him) said, "Allah is one. Do not pray to these idols. They cannot help you. If you pray to Allah, the only God, then He will help you, give you more food and gardens and children, and make you happy after death. Believe me and follow what I am saying, otherwise I fear that Allah may punish you. They said, "We are already rich. We have big stone houses. If Allah is so great, why does He not send angels? You are only a man like us. You want us to follow you so that you can become powerful. You are a liar. You want to cheat us." Nooh (peace be on him) talked to the leaders of the people privately. He also gave warnings in public.

Nooh (peace be on him) tried his best. Allah had granted him long life. Till he was 600 years old he tried. But only a few people believed him. Even his wife did not believe him.

At last the leaders planned to kill him because they saw that the number of believers had increased. They thought he was going to take away their power.

Then Nooh (peace be on him) prayed, "O Allah, these people are wicked. I have tried for such a long time. They do not want the believers to pray. They cause them all sorts of hardship. They do not give them jobs. They try to starve them. Now they are trying to kill me and every believer. O Allah, punish them. Keep only the believers alive."

Allah listened to his prayer. He told him to make a huge boat known as an 'Ark'. Nooh (peace be on him) and his followers made it with big planks of wood and covered the joints with fibre of the palm tree.

When they were making it, the leaders and other rich men would come and laugh at them. They lived in a beautiful, high land, far far away from the ocean. They could not understand how such an Ark could be necessary. They said, "Nooh and his followers are mad people; let them do what they like."

The Flood

When the boat was ready Allah gave an order, "O Nooh, ask all the believers to go on to the Ark. Put one pair each of all animals and birds on the boat." All the believers went in. But Nooh's wife and one of their sons, whose name was Kenan, did not come. They did not believe in Allah. Nooh (peace be on him) also took food and water. His three other sons, Ham, Sham and Yafes, were believers. They went with him.

Then Allah gave His orders. Fountains of water gushed out of the dry land. Floods of rain poured down from Heaven. The sea swelled, drowning everything.

For days this went on. Nooh (peace be on him) and the believers were on the Ark that was now floating on the sea. He saw his son Kenan rushing to the hill top. He shouted, "O my son, come to the Ark. Save thyself." His son shouted back, "I am going to the top of the hill. That is the safest place."

"O fool," Nooh (peace be on him) said, "no place is safe. Will you not believe?" But his son did not listen. He was drowned in the waves.

After days and months when nothing but salty water was seen and all living things had died, Allah gave orders. The rains stopped. The sea shrank back. The land drank up the water.

Nooh's Ark landed on Mount Judi.

Nooh (peace be on him) was sorry for his son's death and said, "O Allah, you had promised to save my relatives."

Allah said, "He was not one of you. Forget him. He was an unbeliever. You will commit sin if you pray for him. You had asked for all unbelievers to be wiped out. Why then pray for one unbeliever just because he was your son?"

Nooh (peace be on him) prayed for Allah's forgiveness.

Allah said, "Now you can live happily with your followers. I bless them and those of your children's children who will remain in the right path."

Nooh (peace be on him) lived for 350 more years and died at the age of 950. His followers did not have any children. All men and women now living on the Earth are said to be the descendants of his three sons, Ham, Sham and Yafes. That is why Nooh (peace be on him) is known as Second Adam.

It is said that till Nooh (peace be on him) all human beings were of one colour and one race. But these three sons were of three colours. Ham was black, Sham was white and Yafes was yellow. Ham's children went to Africa, Sham's children to Europe and Yafes's children towards China. In the Middle East their children got mixed. That is how we get black races in Africa, white races in Europe, yellow races in China and mixed races in the Middle East and the rest of the world.

Ibrahim
(peace be on him)

Trial by Fire

Nooh's Ark had stopped at Mount Judi which was far to the north of Mesopotamia or Iraq. Hundreds of years after that great flood the children and great grandchildren of Nooh (peace be on him) spread all through the land. There sprang up a great kingdom ruled by those who called themselves Chaldeans. Their capital was in Babylonia or Ur. After a time they had a king who became very rich and powerful. His name was Nimrod. The Chaldeans believed that there was one great God but only gods and goddesses could go near Him. They used to build these gods and goddesses out of stone and pray to them. Among them there was a man called Azar — who was a descendant of Sham. He had a son whose name was Ibrahim (peace be on him).

Ibrahim (peace be on him) was an intelligent young boy. As he grew up he could not believe that these gods and goddesses could help anyone. They did not talk to him. They could not move. And they were made by men.

He was so worried that he thought and thought. One night he looked at the sky and saw stars and thought they must be gods. But when the Moon rose they almost faded. So he thought the Moon must be the Great God. But the Moon set. So he said, "God can never die, and can never go away. He cannot set." When the Sun rose he thought, "Now I have found the Great God." But when the Sun also set he felt, "God is He who has made the Sun, the Moon and the Stars." Gradually he became more and more certain. God made him strong in his faith and gave him deep knowledge.

Ibrahim (peace be on him) one day went to the market place, called all the people and asked them, "To whom do you pray?"

They said, "To these idols."

He said, "Do they listen to you when you call on them? Do they do any good or harm to you?"

"No," they said, "but because our forefathers prayed to them, we do so also."

"Then you are wrong and your fathers and forefathers were wrong to worship them. Only the Great God can help. He has made the Sky and the Sun and the Moon. So those gods and goddesses are my enemies. God guides me, gives me food and drink. He will take me away. I hope He will forgive me and put me in Heaven. Those who will not pray to God will be put into the fire of Hell. O God, save me and my father from that fire."

He also told his father not to pray to idols.

His father got angry. "What!" he thought, "a young man comes and tells me to give up my faith. And I am his father. I shall teach him a lesson."

He said, "Ibrahim, you want me to give up what my father and his forefathers believed in. You have become insolent. If you say this again I shall punish you severely."

Ibrahim (peace be on him) was sorry for him. He said, "I shall pray to God for you so that you may become good."

One day when all the people had gone to a big market Ibrahim (peace be on him) took a hammer and broke all the idols except the largest one. He left the hammer hanging from the neck of that one.

When the people came back they saw what had happened. They were very angry. Someone said, "There is a young man called Ibrahim. He was telling us one day to give up our gods. He must have done this mischief. Let us go to Azar's house."

They rushed to Azar's house, called Ibrahim (peace be on him) and asked him, "Have you done this?"

He said, "Why are you accusing me? Why don't you ask the Great idol. He must know the truth."

They felt ashamed. Then one of them said, "But you know they can't talk or see or hear."

"But still you worship them — even when they can't help you?"

"O then, you are surely the one to blame. Come along. We must take you to the King. He will punish you."

They took him to Nimrod. Nimrod asked him, "Why do you ask us to pray to the Great God?"

He said, "He gives you life and death."

Nimrod said, "I am the master here. I give life and I kill whomever I like."

Ibrahim (peace be on him) said, "All right, the sun rises in the East, tell the Sun to rise from the West".

But Nimrod knew he could not do that. He then cleverly said, "All right, if your God is so powerful, if He is the master, if He is going to bring you to Paradise after death, let Him save you now. I shall throw you into a great fire." He ordered that a great fire should be lit and that Ibrahim (peace be on him) should be thrown into it from a high rock.

A great fire was lit. Ibrahim (peace be on him) knew that none but God could help him. He forgot the world. He started praying to God. God then ordered the Fire, "Be a soft bed of flowers when Ibrahim falls."

The Fire was changed into a soft bed of flowers. All men and women were amazed. They could not believe their eyes. But for fear of the King many would not follow Ibrahim (peace be on him).

But the King and some leaders thought he was a great magician. They allowed him to stay there and move freely. But secretly they tried to kill him or do some harm to him and to those who followed him. But all the time God saved him.

One day Allah told him, "This land is cursed. Rise and go to Canaan. I have blessed that land. There your people will prosper."

Ibrahim (peace be on him) then went with his followers all the way from Assyria to Canaan. His brother's son, Loot (Lot), went with him. There, beside the river Jordan, he found a wonderful land, green and rich.

Ismail and Zamzam

Ibrahim (peace be on him) married Sarah but they had no children. As he was growing older, with the permission of Sarah he married Hajar, their slave girl. He had a son by her. His name was Ismail. When Sarah saw that Ibrahim (peace be on him) was very fond of his son, she became jealous of Hajar. This made their life unhappy. Ibrahim (peace be on him) did not know what to do.

When Ismail was only a few months old Allah ordered Ibrahim (peace be on him) to go to Mecca (which was at that time known as Bakka) and leave Hajar and Ismail at that place. Ibrahim (peace be on him) brought them all the way from Canaan to Bakka. But they found a hilly, barren land. In that valley they saw a mound, the mound under which was hidden the broken house of Allah built by Adam. He did not see the house as it was covered with sand. He found the place lonely and dry, without any water. But he had to obey Allah. He left Hajar and Ismail with a bag of dates and a leather bottle full of water. When he was going away Hajar was surprised. She did not know that he would leave them like this. She asked him, "O Ibrahim, where are you going, leaving us in this desert? There is no one here and nothing to eat or drink."

He did not turn back. She then asked him, "Has Allah ordered you to do this or are you doing it yourself?"

He said, "It is Allah's command."

"Then," she said, "He will not let us die."

With firmness and courage she sat on a stone and prayed to Allah for help. Alone, all, all alone she sat.

She suckled the child and drank the water. But when there was no water for her to drink she felt thirsty. Her throat got very dry. She must get some water or she would die. The child was crying. She could not go very far. She rushed to the nearby hill later on known as Safa to see if there was any water or anyone anywhere to help her. She saw no one and she did not find any water.

Then she ran to the other hill later on known as Marwa and found nobody and saw no water. Thus she ran seven times praying to Allah for help. Then she heard someone calling her. She looked at her son and saw an angel pointing at his feet. What joy! There she saw a fountain gushing out of the ground! There was water. She ran. She drank that water. She filled the bottle and dug a well and called it Zamzam. She and Ismail then began to live beside Zamzam.

The Sacrifice of Ismail

Hajar and her child lived beside the well all by themselves. Then one day an Arab tribe called Jurhum came down from the north. They were of Yemen and of the race of Sham, one of the sons of Nooh (peace be on him). When they saw a bird circling they knew that there was water there. Their leaders went down to the valley and met Hajar. With her permission they settled there. They sent some of their men to call other people of the tribe. They came and built houses.

Ismail grew up and learnt Arabic. He became one of the Jurhums. But they always admired him for his noble character.

When Ismail was still young, Ibrahim (peace be on him) dreamt that he was ordered by Allah to sacrifice his most precious thing. As Ismail was the person he loved most he knew what Allah wanted.

He went from Canaan to Hijaz. He was happy to see the house of Hajar and Ismail.

He told Ismail of his dream. Ismail said, "O my father, do as you have been ordered to do. If Allah wills, you will find me patient." Ibrahim (peace be on him) told his son to bring a cord and a knife and they both went to Mount Thabir.

On the way Iblis came to them in the shape of a man and said to Ibrahim (peace be on him), "You must have seen Satan in your dream telling you to cut the throat of your son."

Ibrahim (peace be on him) threw a stone at him and said, "Away, you enemy of Man."

Iblis then turned to Ismail and said, "Do you know, my child, that he says that Allah has told him to cut your throat?"

The child said, "Yes, let Allah's will be done. Go away," and he stoned him.

Iblis again tried to persuade him not to go. But Ismail was angry and took many stones and started throwing them at him.

To this day there are the three places where Hajis go and throw stones and think that like Ibrahim (peace be on him) and Ismail they are driving Satan away.

Satan went to Hajar also and said, "O mother of Ismail, Ibrahim will kill your son."

"No," she said, "he loves him."

"But," the Devil said, "he says it is Allah's order."

"Then," she said, "let what Allah has ordered be done."

Satan was defeated by the strength of their faith.

Ibrahim (peace be on him) and Ismail went up Mount Thabir. Ismail said, "Bind my hands and feet so that I cannot move my hands and feet and that my blood does not gush over you. Turn me on my face so that you are not moved by love."

Then when Ibrahim (peace be on him) was about to make the sacrifice, Allah said, "O Ibrahim, you have acted according to your dream. We therefore give you a victim in place of your son."

Ibrahim (peace be on him), who had shut his eyes, opened them and saw a big ram. It ran down the hill to Mina where they caught it and sacrificed it. That is why Muslims sacrifice some animal on the day after Hajj at Mina.

Ibrahim (peace be on him) brought Ismail back to his mother and went back to Canaan.

The Building of the Kaa'ba

Ibrahim (peace be on him) visited Hijaz again. Ismail had then grown up and was a big man and a Prophet. When Ibrahim (peace be on him) came to the place he could not find Hajar or Ismail. He met a young Jurhumi woman in a hut. There were a few goats near the hut. She was Ri'lah, the daughter of Mudad ibn'Amn and the wife of Ismail. She told Ibrahim (peace be on him) that her husband had gone out hunting. The goats were a present to Ismail.

Ri'lah was very good to Ibrahim (peace be on him). She washed his hair and gave him meat to eat.

When Ibrahim (peace be on him) asked her about Hajar she said that she had died some years ago and she lay buried near that place.

When Ismail returned, Ibrahim (peace be on him) told him to help him to build Allah's house there. But where would they build it? They went out and waited for guidance from Allah. Then a dragon-shaped cloud came and its shadow fell on a place on the mound. They started digging the ground and found to their surprise the ruins of the original house that Adam had built.

Here they raised new foundations and built a house of stone. No mortar was used. Stone was laid on stone. It had no roof.

While building the walls Ibrahim (peace be on him) had to stand on a piece of rock which Ismail had brought for him. The marks of his feet were left on this stone. Since they had no ladder Allah made the stone rise and move as the walls got higher and higher. Ibrahim (peace be on him) and Ismail completed building the Kaa'ba. But they did not give it a roof.

Then they wanted to place a stone on the eastern corner from which they would start going round the Kaa'ba. It is said that when Ismail had gone out in search of a unique stone, the bright stone that was on the grave of Adam (peace be on him) in Mount Abu Qubais moved and fitted itself into that corner. It is this bright stone which has become black in course of time, and is at present known as the Black Stone (Hajri Aswad). This stone you can see in the easternmost corner of the Kaa'ba. Hajis start going round the Kaa'ba after kissing that stone.

After building the Kaa'ba they prayed to God. Ibrahim (peace be on him) said, "O Allah, make this town a secure town. I have placed my child here and his children will remain here. Give food and fruits to the believer." Allah said, "Even the unbelievers will enjoy life here and get food here but they will suffer in the after-life."

They also prayed, "O our Lord, accept our prayers, guide us so that we submit to you. Show us the way. Be merciful to us. Raise from our children people who will believe in You and obey You. Raise up a messenger (Rasool) from among these people. Surely Thou art Mighty and Wise."

Allah accepted their prayer. That is why Allah sent Muhammad (peace and blessings of Allah be on him) among these people.

Ibrahim (peace be on him) and Ismail went round the Kaa'ba seven times. Then they ran seven times to Safa and Marwa to commemorate what Hajar had done when Ismail was a little baby. Finally, Ibrahim (peace be on him) bade goodbye to Ismail, his beloved and only son, and went back to Canaan.

Angels Predict the Birth of Ishaq

Ibrahim (peace be on him) had by this time grown quite old. He was then ninety. He had no child by Sarah. She had also grown old.

One day a group of very handsome young men came to his house. As Ibrahim (peace be on him) always used to eat with a guest, he was very glad to have guests. But when he gave the young men food they did not eat. He understood then who they were.

He said, "You are angels. Why has Allah sent you here?"

They said, "We have been sent to destroy Sodom and Gomorrah, for their inhabitants are wicked people."

Ibrahim (peace be on him) remembered that his nephew Loot was a prophet and he was at that place. He said, "But Loot is there!" They said, "We have been ordered to save him and his followers but not his wife. She is a bad woman."

Then they said, "Allah has said that a child will be born to you both."

Sarah laughed bitterly, "My husband is an old man and I am old and dried up."

They said, "But that is Allah's order. Do not lose hope in Allah's mercy."

Ibrahim (peace be on him) said, "Who can lose the hope of Allah's mercy except those who are misguided?"

He also remembered that Allah had told him long ago to go to Canaan where a child would be born to him called Ishaq and a grandson by Ishaq called Yaqub (Jacob).

Later on Ishaq was born.

Destruction of Sodom and Gomorrah

The people of Sodom and Gomorrah were wicked people. They would not listen to Loot's advice. They would not believe in God. They did all kinds of wicked things. Loot (peace be on him) had several times warned them. They had gone beyond all limits. Allah therefore sent angels to destroy them. Those were the angels who met Ibrahim (peace be on him).

When the angels in the form of young men reached the house of Loot (peace be on him) men came running. They wanted to take the young men away. Loot (peace be on him) said, "You must not do this."

At that moment the angels took on their huge shape. They sent Loot (peace be on him) and the believers away. But as Loot's wife was wicked she was not saved.

Then a huge earthquake came and the angels turned the whole city upside down. This happened somewhere near the place known as the Salt Lake (the Dead Sea).

بِّ قَدْ آتَيْتَنِي مِنَ الْمُلْكِ وَعَلَّمْتَنِي مِنْ تَأْوِيلِ الْأَحَادِيثِ

Yusuf
(peace be on him)

Yusuf's Dream

Ishaq (peace be on him) became a prophet and after him his son Yaqub (peace be on him).

Yaqub (peace be on him) had two wives. By his first wife he had ten sons and by the second he had two – Yusuf and Ben-Yamin (peace be on them). Their mothers died. Yusuf (peace be on him) was the most handsome young man ever seen. His father loved him so much that his elder brothers became very jealous. They saw that his father would allow Yusuf (peace be on him) to play with Ben-Yamin only. They thought their father would make Yusuf (peace be on him) King after him. One day Yusuf (peace be on him) had a wonderful dream. He saw that he was on a throne. The Sun, the Moon and eleven stars had come and were bowing low and saluting him.

When he told his father what he had seen, his father said to him, "Do not tell this dream to your brothers. They will try to do you harm. The Devil is our enemy. Allah will teach you how to understand the meaning of dreams. You will therefore find out what this dream means. Allah will shower His blessings on you, just as He did on your ancestors, Ibrahim and Ishaq (peace be on them)".

The Plot by Yusuf's Brothers

In the meantime the brothers were discussing what to do. One of them said, 'Let us kill him or send him away to some other country. Then father will think only of us."

Another said, "No, let us throw him into the well. Then some merchant will pick him up and take him away." Finally they all agreed to do this.

They then went to Yaqub (peace be on him) and said, "O father, you never allow Yusuf to play with us. Why don't you trust us? We do not want anything but good for him. Let him come tomorrow and play with us. We will guard him well."

Yaqub (peace be on him) said, "You will not look after him properly. I fear some wolf will kill him."

"O no, father, you needn't worry at all. We are a strong group. How can a wolf come near us?" They pleaded and pleaded and at last Yaqub (peace be on him) agreed.

Thus they took Yusuf (peace be on him) away. By a trick they pushed him, as if by mistake, into a dry well. Allah told Yusuf (peace be on him) that one day he would be able to tell them what they had done. This gave Yusuf (peace be on him) peace of mind.

His brothers had taken his shirt from him. They killed an animal and soaked the shirt with blood. Then they went weeping to their father.

"O father," they said, "we were playing games and had gone away leaving Yusuf with our goods. When we returned we found that a wolf had eaten him. We found only his shirt and other clothes soaked with blood."

Yaqub (peace be on him) did not believe them. He only said, "This is a serious matter and surely you have done some mischief, but I shall be patient. I shall seek Allah's help in what you are telling me now."

A caravan of merchants was passing by. They sent someone to fetch water from the well. Yusuf (peace be on him) came up with the bucket. They were very pleased to see so handsome a young boy. They hid him amidst their own goods and took him away. Later on they took him to Egypt and sold him for a few pieces of silver to an Egyptian chief, Aziz. As Aziz had no children, he was glad to have Yusuf. Aziz brought him home to his wife and said, "Now we have a young boy."

Yusuf (peace be on him) and Zulaikha

The Egyptian chief was the prime minister of the King, the Pharaoh. His wife Zulaikha was young and beautiful. She fell in love with Yusuf (peace be on him). Months passed by. Yusuf (peace be on him) grew up to be the most handsome man in the world.

But Yusuf (peace be on him) always kept himself away from Zulaikha.

Zulaikha could not tolerate this. One day she called him into her bedroom. As soon as he entered he understood what she wanted. He ran towards the door. She caught hold of his shirt and as he ran away it got torn.

Just at that time Aziz entered the room.

Zulaikha turned pale with fear.

She put the blame on Yusuf (peace be on him).

"How are you going to punish this young man? He had wicked plans against your wife," she said.

Yusuf (peace be on him) denied this. "It is she," he said, "who wanted to ruin me and lead me away from the path of God."

One of her relatives who was there said, "If the shirt is torn in the front, then Yusuf is guilty. If the shirt is torn at the back then Zulaikha is guilty."

Aziz saw that the shirt was torn at the back. He said, "O Yusuf, forget it. This is a snare made by you, woman. O wife, ask forgiveness for this sin."

Days passed. Zulaikha's love for Yusuf (peace be on him) came to be known to other ladies. When Zulaikha heard what they were gossiping about she wanted to teach them a lesson. One day she invited all the important ladies of the city to her house. She gave each a sharp knife and an apple to eat. Then she opened the door and called Yusuf (peace be on him). When he came the ladies were astonished by his beauty. They were so overwhelmed that they all cut their fingers instead of the apples. They all said, "Who is this? He is not a human being. He is an angel."

Zulaikha said, "This is the man about whom you blame me. I did try to lead him astray. He saved himself. Now if he does not come to me I shall send him to prison."

Yusuf prayed to Allah that he might go to prison and be kept away from her. He was sent to prison.

Yusuf (peace be on him) in Prison

In prison Yusuf (peace be on him) met two other prisoners. They had strange dreams.

One of them said, "I saw I was making wine."

24

The other said, "I saw that I was carrying bread on my head and birds were eating from it."

They asked Yusuf (peace be on him) the meaning of their dream.

Yusuf said, "I shall tell you the meaning. But first of all, you should have faith in Allah. Your gods and goddesses are made by you. They are only names. Do not believe in them. Allah alone has power. Believe in Allah." They obeyed him and became Muslim.

Then he told them the meaning of their dreams. "You will pour out wine to your King," he said to the first prisoner.

To the other one he said, "You will hang from the cross. Birds will eat from off your head."

He said to the one who was going to be saved, "Tell your Lord about me." He became the servant of the King but he forgot this request and Yusuf stayed in prison for a few more years.

The King's Dream

The King of Egypt had a strange dream. He called his learned men.

He said, "I saw seven fat cows being eaten up by seven lean ones. I saw seven green ears of corn and seven withered ones. Will you please explain the meaning?"

They thought of so many meanings. But they got confused. Then his servant came to him and said, "I shall tell you the meaning. But give me leave."

He was permitted to leave. He went to Yusuf (peace be on him) and told him of the dream.

Yusuf (peace be on him) said to him, "For seven years you will have very good crops. You will keep them. Then will come seven dreadful years. There will be no crop. You will eat from what you will save. Then will come one year when there will be enough water."

Yusuf (peace be on him) Becomes a Lord in Charge of the Store-house

When the King heard this he asked his servant who had told him the meaning. His servant told him about Yusuf (peace be on him). The

King then wanted to meet Yusuf (peace be on him). Yusuf (peace be on him) said, "Please ask your Lord what the ladies say about me now."

The King said to the ladies, "What do you have to say about your attempt to mislead Yusuf?" They said, "He is innocent."

Then Zulaikha whose husband had died when Yusuf (peace be on him) was in prison got up and said, "I tried to mislead him, but he saved himself. He is always true and virtuous." When Yusuf (peace be on him) heard the report he said, "Now truth has come out. I have never been false to my master. But Allah is merciful and forgiving."

The King said, "Now bring Yusuf to me."

The King spoke to him and then said, "I am giving you a position of authority. You will be near me."

Yusuf (peace be on him) said, "Put me in charge of the store-house." Thus Allah gave Yusuf (peace be on him) power and honour.

Yusuf (peace be on him) and his Brothers

During these seven years Yusuf (peace be on him) stored as much corn as he could. After seven years of good crops the famine started. Everywhere there was famine. The brothers of Yusuf (peace be on him) came to buy corn. They came to him but they did not recognize him. He however recognized them. He gave them what they paid for.

Then he said, "You have a brother by a different mother. Please bring him next year. If you do not do so, you will not get anything, so do not come near me."

They said, "We shall surely try to bring him. We shall try to get the permission of our father."

Yusuf (peace be on him) told his servant secretly, "Put their money and goods in their bags." He did this so that they would come the following year to return the money which had been paid for their corn.

Yusuf (peace be on him) Meets Ben-Yamin

When they arrived home and told their father, he said, "How can I trust you? Have you forgotten what you did to Yusuf?"

He turned away in sorrow.

They said, "O father, unless Ben-Yamin goes we shall not get our corn."

Then they opened their bags and found their goods and money. They rushed to their father.

"O father, he has returned our money. We will get a camel-load of corn this time. Do send Ben-Yamin. We promise to take good care of him."

Yaqub (peace be on him) made them promise not to come back without Ben-Yamin.

Then he told them, "Do not all enter by the same gate or return by the same gate."

But Allah had a different plan.

After Yusuf (peace be on him) had given them corn he told only Ben-Yamin who he was. He then told a servant to put his cup in Ben-Yamin's saddle bag.

As the caravan started, a servant came shouting "The King's cup has been stolen. Stop. We must search you."

"We haven't stolen it. Search if you like. Tell us, if you find it, what is the punishment?"

"Our law says that the thief will be made a slave to the person whose things he has stolen."

They at first searched the luggage of other brothers and then Ben-Yamin's. When they found the cup in Ben-Yamin's saddle-bag, they took Ben-Yamin away.

The brothers were shocked. They were afraid of what would happen if they told their father about this matter. The eldest said, "You know what you promised when you brought Ben-Yamin. You had done a lot of nasty things to Yusuf. So I am going to stay here. I shall not move from here till Allah orders me or my father permits me. You go and tell father what you have seen. Tell him of this theft by Ben-Yamin and call for witnesses if necessary."

All the Family Comes to Egypt

When the remaining brothers went home and told their father, he did not believe them.

"I shall be patient," he said, "But alas, for Yusuf! Oh Yusuf!"

"You will never be able to forget him. You will be ill and bed-ridden." Yaqub (peace be on him) turned to them and said, "I am only telling Allah. I know what you do not know. Go and search for Yusuf and Ben-Yamin and do not lose hope. Only a man without faith loses hope in the mercy of Allah."

Then they went again to Yusuf (peace be on him). He had by this time become the Prime Minister. They did not have enough money so they wanted some corn in charity.

Yusuf (peace be on him) revealed himself. "Do you remember what you did to Yusuf?"

"Are you Yusuf, then?"

"Yes, I am and this is my brother. Allah has been kind to us. Allah gives reward for patience and good deeds."

They said "Allah has chosen you and raised you above us, we are the wrong doers."

Yusuf (peace be on him) forgave them. He had come to know through insight that his father had become blind. So he gave them his shirt and said, "Go and throw this shirt on his face. He will get back his eyesight. Then all of you should come to me."

At the time when they set out for home Yaqub (peace be on him) started saying, "You may think that I am becoming old and childish, but I am not. I can smell the scent of Yusuf."

People said, "It is your same old feeling."

And when the brothers came and threw the shirt on his face and he got back his eyesight, he said, "Did I not tell you that you did not know what I had learnt from Allah?"

His sons asked his forgiveness and requested him to pray to Allah to forgive them for all the wrong they had done. He promised to do so.

When they reached Yusuf's presence, the entire family bowed down to him. Yusuf (peace be on him) raised his parents to his throne and said, "O father, this is how my dream has been fulfilled and how Allah has shown mercy to me."

He then prayed to Allah, "O Lord, Thou hast given me this power and authority and taught me the meaning of language. O Thou the creator of the Heavens and the Earth, Thou art the protector of my life in this world and my life hereafter. Let me die as a Muslim and let me be raised among those who are pious and good."

Musa

(*peace be on him*)

Israelites Suffer in Egypt

Yaqub (peace be on him) and his twelve sons including Yusuf (peace be on him) and Ben-Yamin settled in Egypt. Yaqub (peace be on him) was also called Israel. His children and their descendants were therefore called Israelites (children of Israel).

As Yaqub (peace be on him) had twelve sons, their children formed twelve tribes.

Many, many years passed. Only a few Egyptians became Muslim. The rest were idol-worshippers. The Israelites kept themselves apart. The Egyptians treated them as slaves. They did not want their number to increase. So Pharaoh, the King of the Egyptians, ordered that the male children should be killed as soon as they were born.

Allah at last became merciful to the Israelites. A great prophet, Musa (peace be on him) was born. His mother hid him in a secret room. At last Allah gave her a message in her heart. She therefore put Musa (peace be on him) in a wooden chest. She cast the chest into the river Nile.

By the grace of Allah this chest landed at the steps of the palace of Pharaoh.

Pharaoh's wife, Asiya, was a religious lady. She believed in Allah. When the chest was brought to her she was pleased to see the child. She wanted to adopt him as her son. With the permission of Pharaoh she started to rear him.

But the child refused to suck. This also was Allah's plan. The Queen, therefore, needed a nurse. The sister of Musa (peace be on him) had followed the chest and seen where it had gone. When she found out that they needed a nurse she said to the Queen, "Shall I show you one who will nurse and rear the child?" Thus Allah arranged that the mother of Musa (peace be on him) was appointed as his nurse.

Musa (peace be on him) grew up to be a very learned man. He was also healthy, tall and strong.

Flight from Egypt

One day Musa (peace be on him) saw how an Egyptian was fighting with a Bani-Israelite and was hitting him unjustly. Musa (peace be on him) saw that the Egyptian was unjust. He therefore intervened and hit the Egyptian once only.

Musa (peace be on him) did not want to kill the Egyptian, but he was so strong that his one blow killed him. He knew that this was wrong and sinful. So he prayed to Allah and Allah forgave him. The matter was reported to Pharaoh. Musa (peace be on him) knew that he would be hanged. So he fled.

Marriage

Pharaoh sent his soldiers to catch him. But Musa (peace be on him) escaped. He fled to the Sinai peninsula. It was 300 miles east of Lower Egypt. He came to Madyan. The people were Arabs and not Egyptians. He rested under a tree near a big well.

Many people had come to the well with goats, lambs and camels to give them water. Musa (peace be on him) saw two young women waiting at a distance keeping back their flocks of sheep. They were not getting any chance to draw water. There were too many men.

Musa (peace be on him) asked them, "What is the matter with you?"

They said, "We cannot water our flocks unless the shepherds take their flocks away. We don't have anyone except our father to protect us. But he is very old." Musa (peace be on him) then watered their flocks. They then went away. He prayed to Allah, "O my Lord! I am badly in need of help."

A few minutes later one of the young women came back. She was bashful. She said, "My father wants to give you some reward. He has invited you to our house."

Musa (peace be on him) went to their house. Their father was a Prophet, Shoaib (peace be on him). He listened to his story and said, "It is good that you have escaped from unjust people."

One of the daughters said, "O father, we need a strong, trusty man. Why not employ him?"

The father said, "I want to give you one of my daughters in marriage. The condition is that you will serve me for eight years. It will be good if you stay for ten years but I do not want to make things difficult for you. You will see that I am a righteous man."

Musa (peace be on him) agreed, "Let there be no ill-will. I shall try to fulfil either of the two terms. May Allah be our witness."

The Divine Call

The ten years were over. Musa (peace be on him) took his family with him and went out in search of a suitable place to live.

On the way they saw a fire. Musa (peace be on him) said to his family, "You stay here. I shall go to that fire and we may get a piece of burning wood so that we may make a fire also. There will be some people there so I shall get some guidance about roads and cities."

When he came to the fire, he heard a Voice, "Musa, I am Your Lord. Take off your shoes. You are in the sacred valley of Tuwa. I have chosen you. Listen then. I am Allah. There is no God but Me. Worship Me only. Establish prayer in order to remember Me.

Surely the Final Hour is coming when everyone will get what he earns by his work. I have kept the time of that Hour hidden.

Therefore those who do not believe, let them not mislead you."

Musa (peace be on him) stood awestruck.

Allah asked him, "What is in your right hand, Musa?"

"It is my stick. I lean on it. I beat fodder with it for my flocks. I also use it for other purposes."

Allah said, "Throw it, O Musa."

He threw it and it became a snake and moved.

Allah said, "Seize it. Don't be afraid. We shall give it its old form."

Musa (peace be on him) seized it. It became a stick again.

Allah then said, "Draw your hand close to your body and then hold it out. It will be white and shining. These are therefore two of our Greater signs for you."

Allah then ordered him, "Now go to Pharaoh. He has gone beyond all bounds."

33

Musa (peace be on him) prayed to Allah, "O my Lord! Make my heart large with wisdom. Make this task given by You easy for me. Make me able to speak smoothly and not stammer, so that they may understand what I say. Also make my brother Haroon my helper so that he may give strength to me and share my work and sing Your praises with me all the time."

Allah granted his prayers. He also told him how He gave the idea to his mother and how his mother became his nurse, how He saved him from the anger of Pharaoh and how He had brought him here.

"I have prepared you for My service. Now both of you should go and speak mildly to Pharaoh."

Musa (peace be on him) said, "I am afraid Pharaoh may say and do evil things."

"Do not be afraid," Allah said, "tell him, 'We are Allah's prophets. Believe and obey Allah. Those who reject Him will suffer. Send the Israelites away in peace. Do not torture them.'"

Musa (peace be on him), Pharaoh and the Magicians

Musa and Haroon (peace be on them) conveyed Allah's message to the Pharaoh. He listened and then said, "O Musa, who is the Lord of you two?"

He said, "Our Lord is the Creator who gave form and nature to everything and then gave guidance to every created thing."

Pharaoh then said, "What has happened to earlier people?"

Musa (peace be on him) replied, "Allah alone knows their condition and He has kept them recorded. He never commits a mistake. He never forgets. He has made the Earth for you like a carpet under your feet. He sends down rain for you and you get crops and fruits."

Musa (peace be on him) showed him the two signs. But Pharaoh thought that it was magic. He said, "O Musa, have you decided to drive us out of our land with your magic? We also have powerful magic. Let us decide on a time for a contest."

Musa (peace be on him) suggested their Day of Festival. As the people of the city would come out on that day, this was the best occasion.

Pharaoh called his magicians and told them, "He who has the upper hand shall be regarded as the victor in the contest."

All the magicians came. Musa (peace be on him) told them to throw whatever they liked. They threw ropes and rods. These seemed to move towards him.

He began to feel rather afraid. Allah told him, "Do not fear. Throw what is in your hand. It will swallow up everything. You will have the upper hand."

Musa (peace be on him) threw what he had in his hand and the ropes and rods were swallowed up.

The magicians bowed down. They became Muslims.

Pharaoh got angry with them.

He said, "How can you become Muslims without my permission? I shall have your hands and feet cut off and then crucify you. You will then see who can give more lasting punishment — I or Musa's Allah."

Their faith had become strong. "We have seen clear signs. We believe in Allah. Do what you like because you can only do this in this life. May Allah forgive us our faults, and our magic. He is Best and Everlasting."

Five Clear Signs and Pharaoh's Death

Musa (peace be on him) warned Pharaoh. But he did not accept the Faith. To teach him Allah's greatness and power as well as His mercy, Musa (peace be on him) prayed to Allah. He wanted Pharaoh and his group to learn through suffering.

Five types of sufferings came — five clear Signs. First of all came a plague and non-believers started dying. Then they told Musa (peace be on him) to pray to Allah and they promised to be believers. The plague stopped. But they did not become believers.

Then came locusts which ate up the crops. People almost starved. They again asked him to pray. When the locusts went away they still did not believe.

Then lice and frogs invaded the land. There were so many of them that people did not know what to do. Again they made a promise. But again they broke their promise when there was no more trouble.

The waters of the Nile suddenly turned into blood. For days and

months the people suffered. Again they approached Musa (peace be on him). Again they rejected the faith when the trouble had gone.

Each time Pharaoh promised to allow the entire Israelite community to leave. But he did not do so when the trouble was over.

After all these attempts Musa (peace be on him) decided to take the Israelites at night and leave Egypt.

During these years of suffering Allah had protected them. They did not suffer. Now Allah helped them again.

Allah gave inspiration to Musa (peace be on him) and told him what to do. When they reached the Red Sea he struck the water with his stick. The sea divided and a dry path appeared. Through this path the Israelites crossed the sea.

Pharaoh had come in pursuit of them. He and all the soldiers and generals rushed along the path. When all of them were on it, the sea rushed in and covered them up. They all died. Later on their Kingdom passed away and during the days of Sulaiman (peace be on him), Egypt and all the other countries of the East and the West were ruled by him.

Twelve Springs

The Israelites went first to the Sinai peninsula. There they saw some people making idols. They requested Musa (peace be on him) to make gods like these. Musa (peace be on him) got angry. He rebuked them. "Do you want to suffer? Have you forgotten your Allah?"

They left that place. As they went on they felt thirsty. There was no water and the women and children were suffering badly.

Then Allah ordered Musa (peace be on him) to strike the mountain with his stick. He did so. Twelve springs of water gushed out.

Each of the twelve tribes of Israel had one spring for itself. They were satisfied.

Manna and Salwa

They did not have food on the way. Musa (peace be on him) prayed to Allah to send Manna and Salwa for them. This food consisted of honey and birds. But the Israelites were ordered not to kill more than they needed for the day. Most of them did not obey the order. They started killing many birds and started storing food. Allah then sent something into the air. All food stored beyond one night rotted. Before that incident food would never go bad. But because of the sin of greed of the Israelites this punishment has been given to mankind.

They were however getting this food regularly. As they did not like the same food, they asked for onions and other spices and vegetables. Musa (peace be on him) got annoyed and told them to enter a city. They did so and immediately they started to suffer all kinds of hardships. This continued till they repented and promised to obey Allah and therefore obey Musa (peace be on him). Allah forgave them.

How the Murderer was Found Out

Then again they misbehaved. One of the Israelites was murdered. No one gave himself up to the authorities and no one informed Musa (peace be on him) who the murderer was. On Allah's order Musa (peace be on him) told them to sacrifice a cow. They thought it was a joke. When Musa (peace be on him) told them that he was not joking and that it was an order from Allah, they started arguing with him.

At first they said, "All cows are the same to us. What sort of cows should we sacrifice?"

Musa (peace be on him) said, "Allah wants you to sacrifice a cow that is neither too old, nor too young, but of middle age. Now do as you are commanded."

They said, "Please ask the Lord of what colour it should be."

He said, "Allah says: A fawn-coloured heifer, pure and rich in tone, everyone who sees it likes and admires it."

They were still trying to avoid having to sacrifice an animal and said to Musa (peace be on him), "Request the Lord to tell us what type of heifer it should be as they are all alike to us."

He said, "Allah says that it should be a heifer that is not trained to till the soil or water the fields, but sound and without blemish."

They had no choice. They offered a cow in sacrifice though they were not happy to do so.

Then Musa (peace be on him) asked them to touch the dead body with a piece of flesh. They did so. The dead man became alive, pointed at the murderer and died again.

The Law and the Covenant

Musa (peace be on him) went up Mount Sinai to thank Allah. He decided to stay for thirty days but he stayed for forty.

Allah gave him all the laws written in Israelite language on tablets. He wanted the Israelites to promise to follow them strictly. Only then would Allah give them victory and glory in this world and happiness in the Hereafter.

Then Allah told Musa (peace be on him), "O Musa, Samiri has made an idol of a calf and the Israelites are worshipping it. Go and stop them."

Musa (peace be on him) went down in anger and sorrow. How could the Israelites be such ungrateful fools? How could they behave like this? What was his brother Haroon doing? He had left Haroon in charge of the Israelites.

Cow-Worship

When Musa (peace be on him) came down from Mount Sinai he saw the idol of a calf made out of ornaments. He threw it down from the altar the Israelites had made. He caught hold of the beard of Haroon and asked him why he had allowed it.

Haroon said, "O brother, do not be harsh on me. These people would not listen to me. I told them. I warned them that Allah would be angry and you would punish them."

Musa (peace be on him) caught hold of Samiri and said, "What have you to say, O Samiri?"

Samiri said, "I saw the foot of the angel Jibreel, but the others did not. So I took the earth on which his steps had fallen and put that earth inside the idol. That's why the calf bleats."

Musa (peace be on him) then banished him and said, "Your punishment is that you will say, 'Do not touch me.' You shall also suffer in the after-life. And see what I am going to do to your god – the god that you started worshipping."

Musa (peace be on him) threw that cow made of gold into a fire. When it melted he threw the molten image into the sea.

Throughout the rest of his life Samiri had to live alone because if he touched anybody or anybody would touch him, both of them would get a high fever. He lived away from society, an outcast, an untouchable.

The Covenant and the Israelites

The Israelites understood that they had done a wicked thing. They repented and were afraid. They said, "If our Lord does not have mercy upon us and does not forgive us, we shall be ruined."

Musa (peace be on him) prayed first for himself and his brother.

Then he chose seventy elders and went to Mount Sinai. He made them stand at a place a short distance from where he would speak with Allah. He took with him the Tablets that Allah had given him. They heard Allah's order.

But the faith of some of those people was not yet strong. They said, "We shall never believe in you unless we actually see God."

Allah then sent lightning, thunder and an earthquake as a punishment for those people and they all fainted and died.

Musa (peace be on him) prayed, "O my Lord, if You wanted You could have destroyed us long ago. Would You destroy us for the wrong things done and said by those of us who are foolish? This is a trial by you. You want to see who goes astray and You want to lead the righteous in the right path. You are our Protector. Forgive us. Be merciful to us. You are the most forgiving, most merciful. We have turned to You. Give us what is right and good both in this life and in the Hereafter."

Allah forgave them, and revived them but threatened to crush them with a rock if they disobeyed him again. They promised to follow what Allah had ordained. They promised to preserve the Tablets, guard them and obey Allah faithfully. Still some of them were weak in their faith.

Musa and Khidr
(peace be on them)

One day someone asked Musa (peace be on him) "Who is the most learned man now?"

Musa (peace be on him) indicated that he himself was. Allah did not like this and decided to teach him how vast was His store of knowledge. He told him to go to the place where two seas used to meet.

A fish would show him the way. The place where the fish disappeared would be the place where he would meet a man whose name was Khidr. This was the man to whom Allah had given special knowledge, directly from Himself.

Musa (peace be on him) followed the fish that Allah had sent. But as he felt hungry he asked his servant to give him food. He therefore lost track of the fish. Therefore he went back to the place where they had last seen the fish.

There they found Khidr (peace be on him), the servant of God, whom Allah wanted Musa (peace be on him) to meet. Musa (peace be on him) said to him: "May I follow you so that you may teach me something of the special knowledge that you have."

Khidr (peace be on him) said, "You won't have patience with me."

Musa (peace be on him) said, "I shall, in-sha-Allah, be patient and obedient to you."

Khidr (peace be on him) then said, "Then please follow me, on condition that you do not ask me any questions."

So they both walked together. They had to cross a river. A poor ferryman took them across the river in his boat. When they were near the other bank Khidr (peace be on him) made a hole in the boat. Musa (peace be on him) was surprised. He said, "Have you made a hole to drown people in the boat?"

Khidr (peace be on him) said, "Didn't I tell you that you would not be able to tolerate what I would do?"

Musa (peace be on him) asked his forgiveness for forgetting his promise.

Then they went on and met a young boy. Khidr (peace be on him) killed him.

Musa (peace be on him) said, "You have done an extremely wicked thing; that boy was innocent. Have you killed someone who has done no harm to anyone?"

Khidr (peace be on him) said, "Didn't I tell you that you would not be able to stay with me?"

Musa (peace be on him) said, "Do not keep me with you if I question again."

They went on and came to a village. The people of that village were wicked. Khidr and Musa (peace be on them) asked them for some food. The villagers refused to give them any.

There was a house whose wall was falling down. Khidr (peace be on him) repaired it and set it up straight.

Musa (peace be on him) said, "If you wanted, you could have got something for this work."

Khidr (peace be on him) said, "This is the time for us to part. But I shall tell you why I did all that you saw.

"The boat belonged to some poor man. But the ruler of that Kingdom was taking away all the good boats. That is why I made it unfit for service.

"The young boy would have become a bad man. His parents were religious. But they would have become corrupt for the love of this child. Allah will now give them a better son in exchange for this one.

"The wall belongs to two orphans. Beneath it is some treasure for them. Their father was a good man. Therefore Allah decided that when they grew up they should get that wealth. I did it because Allah wanted me to repair the wall.

"These are the reasons for all that I have done."

Then they parted company. Musa (peace be on him) understood that there are many kinds of knowledge and Allah grants some kind of knowledge to some people and other kinds of knowledge to others.

Last Days

Musa (peace be on him) was living in the Sinai peninsula with the Israelites. But Allah had promised them a beautiful land if they would follow the law and accept whatever Allah gave them.

At long last Musa (peace be on him) organised a party of twelve people from twelve tribes. They went round and found Canaan. They saw that the people who lived there were tall and strong. But these were unbelievers. Musa (peace be on him) wanted to enter Canaan. Two of the twelve supported him. But the rest did not.

They said, "O Musa! so long as those people are there we shall never be able to enter. You and your God should fight and we will sit here and watch."

Musa (peace be on him) was disappointed. At last when he failed to persuade them, he prayed, "Allah, I have power only over myself and my brother. Separate us from these rebellious people."

Allah said, "In this case they shall not possess the land for forty years. They will move about here and there. Do not be sorry for those who rebel."

As a result Musa (peace be on him) could not enter Canaan either and died before that period of forty years had ended.

Dawood
(peace be on him)

The Israelites and Their Fate

Yusuf (peace be on him) took his father Israel Yaqub (peace be on him) and his eleven brothers to Egypt. Musa (peace be on him) saved their children, the Israelites, from slavery and brought them to Sinai. But they did not listen to his orders. They therefore could not enter the promised land. Later on they repented and were given victory by Allah. Thus they entered the promised land and conquered the Canaanites. They preserved and honoured the Tablets that Musa (peace be on him) had brought and Allah granted them His blessings. These Tablets were put in a chest. It was called the Ark of the Covenant.

Repeatedly they were attacked by unbelievers and they had to fight. Sometimes they themselves misbehaved. They did not follow the Covenant so Allah punished them.

Jaloot and Dawood (peace be on him)

Once the Philistines attacked them. Instead of uniting and repenting they brought out the Ark of the Covenant. They thought the Ark would save them. But as they were corrupt the Philistines defeated them and took the Ark away.

Allah thus taught them a lesson. If they had obeyed the Covenant and behaved rightly Allah would have given them victory. As they did not do so, they could not save themselves simply by showing respect to the Ark.

But the Philistines also suffered because they took away the Ark.

Many years later the Israelites went to their Prophet Samuel (peace be on him). They asked him to give them a King. He knew that they were thinking that Kingship alone would save them. He warned them that that was not enough. Many of them would not follow the right path. However he made Talut of the tribe of Ben-Yamin, their King. Many members of other tribes protested.

They said, "He is not rich or powerful. We are powerful. Why are we not chosen?"

Samuel (peace be on him) said, "He is physically the strongest man. He is also the most learned among you."

As they were not satisfied, prophet Samuel prayed and Allah showed the third sign. He said, "The Ark which you have lost will be brought by angels to Talut." When they saw this, they accepted him as their king.

Then Talut went out to fight the unbelievers. He also wanted to test their faith and their obedience to him. On their way was a river which they had to cross.

He told them, "If anyone drinks of its water, he is not one of us. You are allowed to sip only out of your palms."

Except for a few, most of the Israelites drank deeply. Most people were left behind.

Talut therefore crossed the river with a handful of soldiers. Dawood (peace be on him) was one of them; he was then a young shepherd boy.

The commander of the Philistines was a huge, giant-like man called Jaloot. Many said, "We cannot succeed against such as he."

But a few said, "Allah has often given victory to a small force, Allah is with us."

Then they prayed to Allah, "Our Lord! make us strong. Make our steps firm. Help us against the unbelievers."

Jaloot laughed when he saw such a small band of soldiers. He challenged any one of them to fight with him. They all hesitated.

Young Dawood (peace be on him) came forward. Talut asked him to wear armour and to take a sword.

Dawood (peace be on him) said he had never worn armour or used a sword. He would fight with the shepherd's sling. He had collected some smooth pebbles at the stream.

Jaloot was surprised to see such a young boy coming forward to fight him. But before he could do anything Dawood (peace be on him) sent a pebble flying from his sling. It went right through the left eye of Jaloot. It hit his brain and killed him. He fell down dead. Dawood then took the sword and cut off his head.

The Philistines were terror-struck. They started to flee. The small band began to kill them. They routed the whole army. That is how Allah grants victory to those who have faith.

Dawood (peace be on him) becomes King and Prophet

Allah chose Dawood (peace be on him) and gave him wisdom. He became a prophet. Allah revealed to him knowledge through the verses which formed *Zabur*. He used to sing them. Birds and hills celebrated Allah's praises with him.

Allah also made him the great King of all the Israelite tribes.

Allah also taught him how to melt iron and make coats of steel.

His Judgement

Dawood (peace be on him) was wise and just. One day a shepherd complained that his neighbour, a shepherd, had not taken proper care. The neighbour's sheep went into his field and ate up the crop. Dawood (peace be on him) decided that the neighbour should give the shepherd who had lost his crop all his sheep.

Sulaiman (peace be on him), the son of Dawood (peace be on him), was a young boy. But Allah gave him a better idea than that of his father. The loss was not of the field, only of the crop. Therefore the shepherd should keep his neighbour's sheep until the loss he had suffered had been repaid from the milk and other products of the sheep. Dawood (peace be on him) liked the judgement and gave that verdict.

This also shows how careful and selfless Dawood (peace be on him) was. He accepted the judgement of a young boy.

Allah therefore told him, "O Dawood, we have made you a Vicegerent on earth. Judge between man and man in truth and justice. Do not follow lusts because they will mislead you. Those who are misled will suffer severely on the day of judgement."

Allah kept for him a beautiful place in heaven.

Sulaiman
(peace be on him)

The Great King

Sulaiman (peace be on him) was the wise son of a wise father, Dawood (peace be on him). After Dawood (peace be on him), he became the Prophet and the King.

Allah loved him so much that He made him the greatest ruler of the world. He conquered Egypt. The Prophecy of Musa (peace be on him) was fulfilled. His kingdom spread as far as Ethiopia in Africa, to the southernmost tip of the Arab peninsula, Yemen, to Syria in the North and how far to the East we do not know.

Sulaiman (peace be on him) prayed to Allah, "Allah, please grant me a kingdom the like of which no one has seen before nor will anyone ever see again." Allah granted his prayer.

Allah gave him command over Jinns — both the good and the evil ones. He also gave him power over wind and water and fire and earth. They all obeyed his orders. Birds and animals were under his command. He could understand their language and talk to them.

Sulaiman (peace be on him) Sends a Message to Bilquis

Sulamain (peace be on him) had a large army. There were men, Jinns and even birds with him. They used to move in ranks in an orderly manner.

Once he decided to go out with his soldiers but when he went to see the troops he found that the Hoopoe bird was missing. He was angry.

He said, "If he comes without giving a good reason for his absence, I shall punish him or even execute him."

When the bird came back it said, "I went to visit countries which you have never seen. I wanted to see what the people do. I went to Saba (Sheba). There I found a great Queen ruling. The people there have forgotten Allah. They worship the Sun. The Queen has a wonderful throne and she rules with full authority."

Sulaiman (peace be on him) said, "I shall see whether you are speaking the truth. Take this letter. Drop it before her."

When Bilquis, the Queen of Saba, got the letter she called together her advisers, the chiefs of the country, and asked them what she should do.

They said, "We are strong. We should not bow down to Sulaiman."

Bilquis was wise. She said, "War is a very bad thing. When soldiers come, then the chiefs are insulted, society is upset and women are taken away. Instead of fighting let us send a messenger with gifts."

When Sulaiman (peace be on him) received the gifts he sent richer things back and sent Bilquis through the messenger an invitation to visit him.

The Throne of Bilquis

In the meantime Sulaiman (peace be on him) wanted to teach Bilquis a lesson. He asked his courtiers and followers, "Is there anyone who can bring Bilquis's throne here immediately?"

An Ifrit said, "I can bring it before you leave this place."

A wise saint said, "You will get it in the twinkling of an eye."

And it was there even before the sentence was completed. This was done through the great spiritual power granted by Allah.

Sulaiman (peace be on him) said, "Will someone please change its colour and some of the decorations on the throne so that I can test Bilquis." This was also done.

Bilquis and Sulaiman (peace be on him)

When Bilquis came, Sulaiman (peace be on him) showed her the throne and asked whether this was her throne. She said, "My throne was almost like this."

He then wanted to show her the wealth and greatness that Allah had given him. He requested her to enter his palace. The floor appeared to her to be a lake full of water. She started raising her skirt until her legs could be seen.

Sulaiman (peace be on him) said to her, "Don't be afraid. It is not water. The floor is made of glass."

She was overwhelmed with wonder. She bowed down to Allah and became a Muslim.

Sulaiman (peace be on him) then married her.

Sulaiman (peace be on him) and the Ants

Once Sulaiman (peace be on him) was out with his soldiers. He came to a valley full of ants.

One of the ants called other ants and said, "Go underground. Take shelter. The Prophet Sulaiman is coming. You will get crushed under his feet."

Sulaiman (peace be on him) heard what the ant said and smiled. He praised Allah for all the power Allah had given him.

The Temple of Sulaiman (peace be on him)

Towards the end of his life Sulaiman (peace be on him) decided to build a huge place of worship. Jinns, good and evil, worked on it. They were not allowed to leave the work. Along with them worked the believers. He himself used to supervise.

Allah had given him ability. He gave directions. Beautiful, huge arches were built. Huge blocks of stones were properly cut and shaped. Basins were made as large as reservoirs. Huge cauldrons were made and fixed in their places.

One day he was standing leaning on his stick watching them all at work. Allah decided to take his life away. But at the same time He wanted the work to be finished. So He kept him standing as if Sulaiman (peace be on him) was awake and watching them.

When the work was over, Allah ordered little earth worms to eat up the stick. After some time the stick broke and the body of Sulaiman (peace be on him) fell. Only then did the jinns know that he had died long ago.

This was the most famous temple of Sulaiman (peace be on him) and the Jews used to turn towards this in order to pray.

إن مثل عيسى عند الله كمثل آدم

Isa
(peace be on him)

Condition of Israelites

The Israelites had become the rulers of the world during the days of
Sulaiman (peace be on him). Afterwards again and again they suffered
because of their misdeeds. Many Prophets arose in that family. Some of
the good people took shelter in the hills and jungles in order to lead a
life of purity. Some became monks and lived a life of chastity. They
would train some good people and then allow them to go back to
society. The Romans conquered Jerusalem and what is known as
Palestine. Their empire extended to Egypt, the northern end of Saudi
Arabia and to Persia. The Israelites lived as an unhappy people. Allah
then decided to send to them one great Prophet, Isa (peace be on him).

Birth and Growth of Mariam
(may Allah be pleased with her)

The mother of Isa (peace be on him) was Mariam. Her father was Imran,
her mother, Hannah. Allah chose this Imran family for His special
blessings.

When Hannah was going to have a baby she prayed to Allah, "Allah,
I dedicate this child to you. Keep it safe from Satan. Make it pure and
chaste and good."

She had expected a male child. But she got a girl. However, as she
had dedicated the child to Allah, the child had to be reared as a special
servant of Allah. Relatives cast lots to find out who should be in charge
of the spiritual training of the child. Zakariya, a priest and the husband
of Hannah's cousin, was chosen.

As she grew up Mariam was taken away from her mother and given
a room inside a temple. Whenever Zakariya would go to see her, he
found that she had food and drink.

"Where do you get these from?" asked Zakariya.
"I get them directly from Allah," answered Mariam.
Zakariya was surprised. But he believed what she said.

Birth of Yahya (peace be on him)

When Zakariya saw this miracle, he remembered that he was childless. He prayed to Allah, "O Allah, give me a son. I shall dedicate him to you."

The Angels told him, "Allah has granted your prayer. You will have a good, pious son. His name will be Yahya. He will be a prophet."

"Allah," he said, "I am very old. My wife is old. How can we have a son? May I then have some signs by which I shall know this?" The Angels said, "Yes, for three days you will not speak. This will indicate that Yahya is coming."

Thus Yahya (peace be on him), a cousin of Mariam, was born. He would be the person to support and help Isa (peace be on him).

Birth of Isa (peace be on him)

Allah had chosen Mariam for a great miracle. He wanted to show man that He could do what He liked. He also wanted to let men see that He could make a child without a father so that man might know that he could make Adam (peace be on him) without a father or a mother.

Mariam (Allah be pleased with her) grew to be a beautiful young lady. One day she saw the angel Jibreel (peace be on him) in the form of a man. She was afraid. He told her not to be afraid. "I am an angel sent by Allah, I have come to announce that Allah has decided to give you a child who will be his servant."

She was surprised. "How can it be?" she said. "No man has ever touched me."

He said, "Allah can do whatever he wants. Your son has been named by Allah, Isa Masih Ibn-Mariam. He is to be strengthened by the holy spirit of Allah. Allah is sending him as a prophet. He will be a Sign of Allah to mankind and of the blessings of Allah for the whole of creation."

"What answer shall I give to people when they will ask about him?"

Jibreel (peace be on him) told her, "You need not give any reply. Tell them by a sign that you are fasting and point to the child. Allah will grant this child speech. He will reply."

Jibreel (peace be on him) then transferred, by the grace of Allah, the Spirit to her.

Thus she conceived. Thus Allah showed to the entire world His power, His grace and His mercy.

When at last, the usual period was over she went away to a distant lonely place. She felt so much pain that she cried, "O Allah, were I dead before this."

In the meantime the child was born. She heard a voice from under her saying, "Here under you is a spring of water. Drink it and clean yourself. Shake that date tree. Ripe fruits will fall. Eat and be strong."

A spring gushed out. And she drank and washed. She took hold of the tree and shook it. Ripe dates fell. She ate and Allah gave her strength.

Child Isa (peace be on him) Defends his Mother

Mariam (may Allah be pleased with her) returned with the child. People were surprised, shocked and bewildered.

"How could this happen? O Mariam! O sister of Haroon! Your father was a pious man. Your mother was not unchaste. But what is this! How could you fall so low?"

As instructed by Allah she did not speak. She pointed at the child, meaning that they should talk to him.

"He is a little baby. How can we talk to him?"

The child then spoke.

Awe-struck, they listened in absolute silence.

"I am Isa Masih, I am a servant of Allah. I have been sent to you with a message. I shall establish prayer and chastity. Allah has showered peace and blessings on the day I was born, on the day I shall die and on the day I shall rise again. I am obedient to my mother and I shall never give any pain to her. So follow me and be on the right path."

All evil tongues were silent.

His Miracles

Each prophet is granted some special power. Even before the birth of Isa (peace be on him), when the angels told his mother that he would come, they also told her of his powers.

They said, "Even as a baby he will be able to speak. He will be able to cure the leper and bring light to blind eyes. He will be able to give life to the dead. He will make a bird with clay and give it life so that it will fly. All these things he will be able to do by the permission of Allah." As Isa (peace be on him) grew up, he was trained by Yahya (peace be on him).

On many occasions, many miracles took place. Poor and helpless people used to come to him every day. He would cure them. One day he called Lazarus and he came out of his grave, alive! He showed these miracles only to convince people of his Prophethood and to make them believe in what he was preaching. Even then a large number of Israelites did not accept him. They were the people who complained against him to the Roman governor.

A Table with Food from Heaven

It was during this time that a new miracle happened. The disciples of Isa (peace be on him) appealed to him to bring down a table full of food sent from Heaven. They said, "We do not want this in order to believe in Allah's power. We are begging you to get this for us because it will make us realize that you are speaking the truth. We also want to be a witness to the miracle."

Isa (peace be on him) prayed and Allah granted his prayer. A table full of Heavenly food came down. Isa (peace be on him) asked his disciples to eat only as much as was necessary.

Isa (peace be on him) is Taken Up

Some of the Israelites did not believe in Isa (peace be on him). They were jealous. They reported lies to the Roman governor against him. At last Judas, one of those disciples who were with him, decided to betray him. Saint Barnabas, one of his closest disciples, has written about this.

Isa (peace be on him) was staying in a disciple's house. Judas had told the Roman soldiers that they should catch the man whom he would kiss on the cheek. He went and kissed Isa (peace be on him). But the whole room became dark and there was confusion. When the room became bright the soldiers caught Judas because Allah had changed his features. He looked like Isa (peace be on him). He protested. He appealed. But the soldiers laughed. They put a crown of thorns on him and said, thinking that he was Isa (peace be on him), "Now you are the King of the Jews."

He was taken to the gallows and crucified.

Most of the disciples of Isa (peace be on him) were either confused or believed that it was Isa (peace be on him) who was crucified. Some of them went and buried him. Later on some of them dug up the grave and took away the dead body and told people that he had gone to Heaven.

But Allah had lifted him up at the time the Roman soldiers had come.

Saint Barnabas, one of his nearest disciples, says in his written account that he was not crucified and that he was alive. He came in the company of angels in order to tell his mother that he was alive so that she could get some peace of mind.

That is why Allah tells the Jews through the *Quran*, that they could not kill him or crucify him. Allah had taken him up and saved him. He would come back.

Return of Isa (peace be on him)

The prophet of Islam, Muhammad (peace and blessings of Allah on him) told his disciples that Isa (peace be on him) would return to this earth in order to kill Dajjal, the terrible unbeliever. After that he would fight and destroy all evil powers and rule the whole world. Every single man and woman alive after all these wars would become a Muslim.

Isa (peace be on him) would rule for forty-five years, marry and have children and die a normal death. He would be buried in the same place where Muhammad (peace and blessings of Allah be on him) lies buried. They would rise together on the Last Day of Judgement.

وما ارسلناك إلا رحمة للعالمين

Muhammad
(peace and blessings of Allah be upon him)

The Last Prophet

When Ibrahim and Isma'il (peace be on them) had finished rebuilding the Kaa'ba, the house of Allah, they stood near it and prayed to Allah, "O Allah, send to the children of our children a Prophet who will make them pure and good, teach them the book of knowledge that you will send down and make them wise."

Allah fulfilled their prayer. He sent Muhammad (peace be upon him). He was the last Prophet and the only Prophet after Isma'il (peace be upon him) in the family line of Isma'il and the only Prophet after Isa (Jesus, peace be upon him). The Prophet Muhammad was born in Makkah on Monday, the twelfth day of the lunar month of *Rabi' al-Awwal* in the year 570 CE (Common Era). One of Isma'il's descendants was called Quraysh, and his tribe was named after him. The Prophet Muhammad (peace be upon him) was born into that tribe.

The Prophet Muhammad's life started with sorrows. His father Abdullah died a few months before his birth. His mother's name was Aminah. He could not enjoy her affection for very long, for she died when he was just six years old. They were returning from Madina where she had gone to visit his father's grave and meet her relatives. On the way home she fell ill and died, and Muhammad (peace be upon him) became an orphan. A slave girl who was with them took Muhammad (peace be upon him) back to Makkah, where his grandfather, Abdul Muttalib, took charge of him. Within two years his grandfather also passed away. Before his death he asked Abu Talib, Abdullah's brother, to take charge of the boy. Till his death Abu Talib protected, guarded and helped Muhammad (peace be upon him). Thus Muhammad's life began with sorrows and losses.

Even before Muhammad (peace be upon him) was born Allah had sent a message to his mother about his great future. Aminah once saw a bright light coming out of her and lighting up the whole world. Some days before her son's birth, she saw an angel in a dream. The angel came down from the sky and said to her: "Glad news to you, O mother of the blessed last Prophet. Your son will be the deliverer of mankind. The name which has been decided upon for him is Ahmad." She therefore named her son Ahmad, which means "the most praised one". After his birth, his grandfather took him to the Kaa'ba and named him Muhammad, "the praised one". Both the words come from the same root. It is the second name by which he is generally known. The name Ahmad also occurs in the Qur'an. Muslims all over the world know both the names and use them when they ask for the blessings of Allah on his soul.

The Cleansing of his Heart

It was an Arab custom in those days to let the babies of good families be looked after by a foster mother. Aminah entrusted Muhammad (peace be upon him) to Halimah, who brought him back to his mother after fostering him for two years. But after pleading with Aminah, Halimah took him back again. The main reason for doing this was that while this child was in Halimah's house, her date trees, her sheep and her camel all thrived and Halimah lived happily.

After Halimah had taken him back from his mother, a strange miracle happened. One day the child was playing in the fields, when all of a sudden he saw two people coming towards him. One held him tightly. The other cut his chest open with a sharp knife, brought out something black from his heart, cleaned it with water, put his heart back in and sewed up his chest. When they were gone, Muhammad (peace be upon him) got up, shaken – but he was quite normal. Was it a vision or a reality? Many Muslim sages explain that this was how Allah purified Muhammad (peace be upon him) of the bad element in human nature. Halimah's daughter saw what was happening and ran to tell Halimah. When Halimah heard from Muhammad (peace be upon him) all that had taken place, she was afraid and returned him to Aminah.

Bahira and the Cloud

When Muhammad was being looked after by Abu Talib another miracle happened. He was now a boy of 12. His uncle Abu Talib was going to Syria in connection with business. Muhammad (peace be upon him) wanted to be with his uncle. Abu Talib took him on the journey. Their trade caravan halted at an oasis near Basra, where a Christian monk named Bahira had a monastery. Bahira saw a low cloud between the sun and the travellers. It was hovering over the oasis where the Arab caravan had halted. He had a manuscript which predicted the coming of the last Prophet, and it described his features. Bahira invited the traders to eat with him. They left Muhammad (peace be upon him) with the animals and the goods. Bahira saw the cloud giving shade to the place where Muhammad (peace be upon him) was. He asked the traders if they had left anyone with the caravan, and after learning that a young boy was there, he requested them to call him.

After the meal Bahira talked to Abu Talib and Muhammad (peace be upon him). Abu Talib wanted to pose as Muhammad's father, perhaps to protect him, but Bahira knew from the manuscript that he was an orphan. When Abu Talib admitted that he was Muhammad's uncle, Bahira told him: "He is the last Prophet. Take your brother's son back to his country. Guard him against his enemies. By God, if they see him and know of him that which I know, they will try to do him harm. Great things are in store for your brother's son." The monk then kissed the 'Seal' of the Last Prophet, a swollen area on the back of Muhammad's shoulder (peace be upon him) about the size of a pigeon's egg which was always shiny as if it was full of light.

When someone asked Bahira how he knew all this, he said, "I saw the trees and stones bowing down to him and the clouds giving him shade."

Bahira also wanted to know about his way of living, and asked Muhammad (peace be upon him) to swear by two idols which were called al-Lat and al-'Uzza. Muhammad (peace be upon him) replied that he would not swear by them, for he did not believe in these idols. When Bahira then asked him to swear in the Name of Allah, he agreed to do so.

Al-Amin – the Trustworthy

Muhammad (peace be upon him) grew up to be a quiet, loveable youth. He came to be known as a truthful, trustworthy young man. He would never betray any trust. Muhammad (peace be upon him) also never broke his word, however difficult it might turn out to be to fulfil his commitment. This was why people would call him "*al-Amin*" – the Trustworthy.

Organising Youth for Peace

Muhammad (peace be upon him) was always very sorry to see the corruption and cruelty in his country. He helped the Makkan tribes to make friends with each other, especially through some influential young people. Their duty was to find ways and means of stopping violence and preserving and maintaining peace, of seeing that justice was done and of helping strangers and travellers who were often cheated and looted. This he succeeded in doing after it was decided to end the long war between the Quraysh and the neighbouring Qais tribe. This war was known as the Battle of Fijar. Peace was made under an agreement known as the Agreement of Fudul, the place where the agreement was made.

Marriage with Khadijah

Khadijah was a rich widow of high social status in Makkah. She appointed him to trade for her because she came to know of his truthfulness and honesty. Khadijah sent her slave Maisarah as an assistant to Muhammad (peace be upon him). The profit from the trade went far beyond Khadijah's expectations, and the slave Maisarah also reported to her on Muhammad's honesty and fair dealings. This convinced her of his greatness. She sent a proposal of marriage to him. Muhammad (peace be upon him) referred the matter to his uncle. He was delighted. The marriage took place. Khadijah was at that time 40 and Muhammad (peace be upon him) was only 25.

Khadijah gave her husband total charge of her business. Muhammad (peace be upon him) did not marry again as long as she was alive. Even though he had other wives later on, his love for Khadijah was foremost in his heart, a love that sometimes made his third wife, 'A'ishah, feel jealous.

Khadijah was the mother of all of Muhammad's children except for one, Ibrahim, who was born of Maria, a slave girl sent to him from the King of Egypt when he was in Madina. Only one daughter by Khadijah, Fatimah, was still alive when he died. As his eldest son was called Qasim, Muhammad (peace be upon him) came to be called "Abul Qasim" – father of Qasim.

Muhammad (peace be upon him) hated it when slaves were ill-treated. It was only after marrying Khadijah that he was able to buy and set some of them free. Khadijah had given him a young slave, Zaid, as a gift. Zaid had been stolen from home by someone who sold him to a Makkan who gave him to Khadijah. When Zaid's father learnt where his son was, he came to claim him. Muhammad (peace be upon him) then told Zaid that he was free to go with his father, but Zaid had become so attached to him that he refused to go. Muhammad (peace be upon him) declared that from that time on he would regard Zaid as his own son. This shows how Muhammad (peace be upon him) treated slaves as his equals.

Illiteracy

Muhammad (peace be upon him) did not receive any formal schooling, and never learnt how to read or write. Before his marriage he was poor, and worked as a shepherd. Later on he was occupied with his trade, family life and meditation. That is why the Muslims say that the Qur'an could not have been made up by Muhammad (peace be upon him), because he could not write, and he never read any books, or studied with any teacher. All the knowledge and wisdom that he had was given to him by Allah.

Seclusion and Meditation for 15 Years

After his marriage to Khadijah, Muhammad (peace be upon him) spent a lot of time in seclusion and meditation in a cave in Mount Hira near Makkah. Sometimes he would be away from home for fifteen days at a time. Otherwise he would be away for a day or two. Khadijah always gave him her wholehearted support. She was convinced of his sincerity, and so she never objected to this retreat. She continued to support what he was doing, even though she was worried about his safety. He used to take only some dried bread, dates and water. Neither she nor their daughter Fatimah disclosed this secret to anyone. Very few details of his experiences at this time are known to us, although we know of the greetings that he would often hear: "Peace be on you, O Messenger of Allah." Muhammad would turn and look for the speaker, but could see no one.

This sort of retreat would not have seemed strange to his tribe because it was a traditional practice among the descendants of Isma'il. In each generation there would be one or two such people. We have learnt from what Muhammad (peace be upon him) said later, that at first he had good dreams, and then visions about the Unseen; and then his eyesight was transformed and he saw with his own eyes the angel Gabriel and other angels.

His Wisdom and Leadership

During this period of meditation, one significant incident took place. When he was 35 years old, the Kaa'ba, the house of Allah that Ibrahim and Isma'il had rebuilt, was damaged by torrential rain and flooding. The tribal leaders dismantled the house, rebuilt it and covered it with a wooden roof. Trouble started when they were about to replace the black stone which had been fixed by Ibrahim and Isma'il at one of its corners. This stone was always regarded with reverence, and it was the practice of all visitors to the Kaa'ba to first kiss the stone and then to walk round the building.

The question arose as to who should put the black stone back in its place. Discussion led to arguments among the tribal leaders, and almost to bloodshed. When they saw Muhammad (peace be upon him) entering the arena, they decided unanimously to ask him to decide what should be done. Muhammad (peace be upon him) accepted this request. He spread his cloak on the ground, and placed the black stone on it. Then he requested all the tribal leaders to hold the edges of the cloak and carry the stone to the Kaa'ba. This they did. Then Muhammad (peace be upon him) raised the stone and placed it in the corner where it was supposed to be. Everyone was satisfied, and bloodshed was avoided.

The First Revelations

When Muhammad (peace be upon him) was 40 years old a strange thing happened while he was meditating in the cave in Mount Hira near Makkah. In the cave he saw someone in a human form who told him, "Read!" Muhammad (peace be upon him) said, "I cannot read." The person embraced him and said again, "Read!" and he repeated, "I cannot read." Again the person pressed Muhammad (peace be upon him) to him, almost to the limit of his endurance, and repeated, "Read!" Muhammad (peace be upon him) again replied, "I cannot read." Then the person pressed him a third time, and said:

Recite: In the Name of your Lord who created,
Created Man from a blood-clot.
Recite: And your Lord is the Most Generous
Who taught by the Pen,
Taught Man what he knew not. (*Qur'an*, 96: 1-5)

Muhammad (peace be upon him) said later that when the person had left him, he felt as though the words which had been recited to him had been written on his heart. He started thinking: "Was it an evil spirit? Am I possessed? Have I become a poet?" Muhammad (peace be upon him) left the cave and started rushing down the hill. He heard a voice "O Muhammad, you are the Messenger of Allah, and I am the angel Gabriel." He looked up and saw the person who had recited the words to him in the cave. Whichever way he turned he saw the angel in front of him. He rushed back home shivering. Khadijah asked him what was wrong, and he told her what had happened. Khadijah assured him, "You are definitely the Prophet, it was surely an angel and not an evil spirit."

Khadijah then went to her cousin Waraqah bin Nawfal, a wise Christian who did not believe in idol worship. He listened to everything Khadijah told him and assured her that she was right.

The next morning Muhammad (peace be upon him) narrated the whole incident to Waraqah. Waraqah said, "You are the Prophet about whom prophecy has been made. The angel that you saw is the same angel who brought messages to other prophets. You will be persecuted and you will have to leave this place. Evil people will drive you out. If I am alive when you are asked to call people to worship Allah then I shall accept you and follow you." But Waraqah died before the Prophet Muhammad (peace be upon him) started preaching.

How the Revelations Used to Come

After this assurance from Waraqah, the Prophet was calm and confident. When revelations started coming, he was able to receive them without any worry. But it was not an easy experience – at times he would almost faint. Following his instructions, his Companions would cover him with a sheet or a blanket. Even during the middle of winter he would get up exhausted, with perspiration all over his face and body. Then he would recite to his Companions the verses which had been revealed to him. These Companions were the first Muslims, after Khadijah. The Prophet mentioned two ways in which the revelations came to him:

> Sometimes it comes to me like the ringing of a bell, and that is the hardest upon me; the ringing dies down when I am awake and I am aware of the message. Sometimes the Angel takes the form of a man and speaks to me and I remember exactly what he says. (Bukhari)

Writing Down and Memorising the Qur'an

The Prophet Muhammad (peace be upon him) later instructed some of his Companions to write down the revelations, as soon as they were revealed, and some of them who had excellent memories to learn them by heart. All these revelations together make up what we know as "the Qur'an". Someone who memorises the whole of the Qur'an by heart is known as a *hafidh* (sometimes written as *hafiz*). Muhammad (peace be upon him) also received instructions through the angel Gabriel as to the order in which the verses should be placed.

Muhammad (peace be upon him) Learns How to Pray

The angel Gabriel also taught Muhammad (peace be upon him) how to wash before praying (*wudu*) in order to purify himself, and how to pray in all the positions: standing, bowing, prostrating and sitting. He taught him to begin the prayer by saying the words which proclaim God's Glory: *Allahu Akbar* (God is most Great), and to repeat these words during the prayer, and the final greeting with which the prayer ends: *Assalamu 'alaikum* (peace be on you). The Prophet then taught Khadijah, and they prayed together. Muslims have prayed in this way ever since.

The First Muslims

After the first revelations there was a period of silence, which made the Prophet Muhammad (peace be upon him) worried. Then came the assurance that Allah had not forsaken him, and he was directed to "declare your Lord's blessing." (*Qur'an*, 93: 11). Only then did he start preaching. He preached first to his own household, then among his nearest relations and then among those he knew. Khadijah was the first person to accept the Prophet's message, the first Muslim.

After Khadijah and their daughter Fatimah had become Muslim, Ali (the Prophet's cousin) and Zaid (the young slave) accepted Islam too. Ali was a son of Abu Talib, and he was ten years old at the time. Muhammad (peace be upon him) had looked after Ali after his marriage with Khadijah. Abu Bakr, a wise and wealthy businessman, became convinced of the truth of Islam when he talked to the Prophet, and he became the first adult male Muslim. He then persuaded a few others to accept Islam. Thus Talha, Uthman and Abdullah ibn Mas'ud joined the ranks of the Prophet's close Companions. Umm Aiman was the first slave girl to become a Muslim. They all used to pray together in secrecy and greet each other with the greeting that the angel Gabriel had taught the Prophet – *Assalamu 'alaikum* (peace be on you).

Within two years Muhammad (peace be upon him) received an order from Allah to openly call everyone to only worship Allah. He called everyone to Safa, one of the two small hills near the Kaaʻba between which Hajar had run looking for help when the Prophet Ibrahim (peace be on him) had first left her there with their baby Ismaʻil in the middle of the desert.

When they had come he said, "If I told you that a big army was coming to attack you from the other side, would you believe me?" All of them said, "Of course. We all know and believe that you always speak the truth." Then he said, "If that is so, then listen to me. Pray to Allah alone. Give up worshipping idols. Give up evil ways. Then you will be successful. If you don't, then you will suffer badly, and it will be too late to do anything to save yourselves."

Most of those who were assembled there did not know what to say. But some were angry and shouted, "You have gone mad!" Abu Lahab, one of the Prophet's uncles, shouted, "May Allah destroy you. Have you called us for this?" He then left and all the others went away.

A few days later the Prophet invited his uncles, cousins and nephews to his house. He said, "I have brought you a great religion. Whoever follows it will have success in this world and in the next world. Is there anyone who wants to help me in this mission?" Only young Ali got up and said that he would. Abu Lahab, the Prophet's uncle, again got angry and walked out. Others kept quiet and silently went away.

Persecution Begins

When the number of Muslims reached 40, the Prophet Muhammad (peace be upon him) went to the Kaaʻba and proclaimed that God is One and that he was God's Prophet. He invited everyone to follow the truth and to give up worshipping idols. Those who refused to believe him regarded this declaration as the biggest insult to their faith and customs. They attacked the Prophet. Harith bin Hala, a new Muslim rushed out of his house to protect the Prophet. He was killed, and so became the first martyr in the history of Islam.

More and more people started entering Islam. The leaders of the Quraysh tribe saw that the Prophet was determined to do what God had asked him to do. At first they ignored him, thinking that he was possessed. But then they found him openly proclaiming his faith. They discovered that some important influential people were listening to him. In order to stop him they told his uncle that they would give him leadership, wealth and the most beautiful woman of Arabia if only he would stop preaching against their gods and goddesses and their way of life. Abu Talib was himself wavering. But the Prophet told his uncle, "Even if they put the sun in my right hand and the moon in my left, I shall not give up what Allah has asked me to do."

This convinced Abu Talib of Muhammad's total commitment and sincerity and so he told Muhammad (peace be upon him) that he would support him. This he did, until his death in the tenth year of the Prophet's mission.

When they failed to tempt the Prophet, the leaders of those who rejected him, of whom Abu Jahl was the most outspoken, increased their taunts and tortures. It was the slaves who suffered most. Bilal, a black slave, who later became a great Companion of the Prophet, was forced to lie on hot sand with heavy stones on his chest and told to renounce Islam. He only cried, "Allah is One, Allah is One!" Abu Bakr bought him from his cruel master and freed him. Other slaves were also tortured. Even women slaves were made to suffer. But they did not give up their faith, nor did their faith weaken. God gave them strength to remain patient.

The Migration to Abyssinia

The torture became almost unbearable. The unbelievers were ready to kill the Muslims and take away their property. The Prophet (peace be upon him) told a group of Muslims to migrate to Abyssinia to seek protection. This migration took place in *Rajab,* the seventh month in the lunar calendar, in the fifth year of the Prophet's mission.

The Quraysh sent two men to Abyssinia and asked king Negus, to send the Muslims back because, they said, they were rebels. King Negus wanted to hear the Muslim's story. This is what Ja'far, the Prophet's cousin, a son of Abu Talib, told the king:

We were a people full of ignorance and immorality, worshipping idols and committing all sorts of evil and injustice, and treating guests badly. The strong among us would exploit the weak. Then Allah sent a Prophet from among us. We knew his lineage, truthfulness, trustworthiness and integrity.

He called us to worship God alone, to testify to His Oneness, and to give up worshipping the stones and idols that our ancestors used to worship. He commanded us to speak the truth, to honour our promises, to respect the ties of kinship, to be good to our neighbours, to abstain from crimes and bloodshed, and to avoid adultery and fornication. He has commanded us not to bear false witness, nor to steal an orphan's property, nor to falsely accuse a married woman of being unfaithful. So we worship Allah only, follow Him in what He has told us is lawful, and avoid what He has forbidden us to do.

That is why our people have attacked us, treated us harshly and tried to make us give up our religion and our worship of God, in order to try and make us go back to immorality and the worship of idols. That is why we seek your protection, so that we may live in justice and peace.

The king listened to these words and then asked the Muslims to recite some of their revelation. Ja'far recited some verses from *Surah Maryam* (Chapter 'Mary'), which speak about the birth of Jesus (peace be upon him). King Negus and his bishops wept. Then king Negus said, "This has definitely come from the same source as the messages that Jesus brought." King Negus then turned to the messengers of the Quraysh and said to them, "You may go. By God I will not hand them over to you; they shall not be betrayed."

The Conversion of 'Umar

The two most powerful opponents of Islam at this time were Abu Jahl and 'Umar. Muhammad (peace be upon him) used to pray to Allah to convert them. Allah informed Muhammad (peace be upon him) through the angel Gabriel that He had accepted part of his prayer and had granted faith to 'Umar. The Prophet received this message on the very day that 'Umar had left his house with a naked sword to kill him. This is what happened: On the way to the Prophet's house, 'Umar met someone who had secretly become a Muslim. When this person heard that 'Umar was out to kill the Prophet, he told him that 'Umar's own sister and brother-in-law had accepted Islam. 'Umar then rushed to his sister's house. There, Khabbab, one of the Prophet's Companions, was reading some verses of the Qur'an with them.

When 'Umar called out to his brother-in-law, they put away the page of the Qur'an, and Khabbab hid himself behind a screen. 'Umar was full of rage. He asked his sister and brother-in-law whether they had become Muslim. When they said "Yes," he started beating his brother-in-law. 'Umar's sister tried to save her husband, but a blow hit her and blood gushed out. This stopped 'Umar. Suddenly something happened to him. He asked to see what they were reading. 'Umar's sister told him defiantly, "You are unclean, I won't give it to you."

They were surprised when 'Umar asked, "Can I be purified?" It seemed that 'Umar was sincere, and so his sister taught him how to do *wudu*, and he did so. The page that was given to 'Umar to read contained the opening verses of *Surah Ta-Ha* (the twentieth Chapter in the Qur'an). The moment 'Umar read it he said, "How beautiful and noble are these words." Khabbab came out from behind the screen when he heard this and said to 'Umar, "O 'Umar, I have hope that Allah has chosen you through the prayer of His Prophet."

"O Khabbab", replied 'Umar, "Where will Muhammad be now, that I may go to him and enter Islam?" Khabbab took him to the Prophet's house. Although the Companions were afraid for his safety, the Prophet (peace be upon him) instructed them to open the door. "O Messenger of Allah", 'Umar said, "I have come to you that I may declare my faith in Allah, and in His Messenger and in what he has brought from Allah." "*Allahu Akbar*! (God is Most Great!)", said the Prophet in such a way that everyone realised that 'Umar had entered Islam. The conversion of 'Umar took place in the sixth year of the Prophet Muhammad's mission, (peace be upon him).

Hamzah Accepts Islam

The next most influential person to accept Islam in the same year was the great warrior, Hamzah, who was one of the Prophet's uncles. Hamzah had gone out hunting, and when he returned, a woman told him that Abu Jahl had taunted Muhammad (peace be upon him) and hit him.

As Muhammad (peace be upon him) was under the protection of his family, Hamzah felt insulted. He rushed to the Kaa'ba, and found Abu Jahl sitting by the small hill of Safa talking to his followers. Hamzah took his bow and hit Abu Jahl hard and then said, "Now know that I also accept Islam and that I shall support Muhammad whole-heartedly. – Be careful!"

Abu Jahl's followers wanted to fight. But Abu Jahl stopped them and told them that Hamzah had hit him because he had hit Muhammad (peace be upon him).

More Persecution: The Boycott

It was after the conversion of 'Umar that the Prophet Muhammad (peace be upon him) persuaded all the new Muslims to go to the house of Allah, the Kaa'ba, and to say their prayers openly. The unbelievers saw this as an act of open defiance against their gods and goddesses but they did not fight the Muslims. Instead they boycotted the Hashimite clan of the Prophet and made the Muslims suffer by driving them out of Makkah.

Abu Jahl succeeded in persuading other tribal chiefs to boycott the family of Hashim, the great grandfather of the Prophet (peace be upon him), and to confine them in a mountain ravine that is now called Shibi Abu Talib. The situation of the Muslims was so difficult that again, some of them went to Abyssinia to find refuge.

However, the boycott did not succeed, although it continued for three years. Secretly many people supported the Muslims and brought them food to prevent them from dying of starvation. Eventually the boycott had to be called off, as serious differences began to arise between the people who supported the Hashimites and those who did not.

Throughout this time the Prophet (peace be upon him), the Hashimite clan and the other believers did not take recourse to fighting. They obeyed Allah's commands, "And bear patiently with what they say, and forsake them graciously," (*Qur'an*, 73: 10), and, "Give respite to the unbelievers; deal with them gently for a while." (*Qur'an*, 86: 17).

The Year of Sorrow

After the boycott had ended, the two greatest supporters of the Prophet, Abu Talib and the Prophet's beloved wife Khadijah died. Muhammad (peace be upon him) called this tenth year of his mission, "The Year of Sorrow". After Abu Talib and Khadijah had died, the situation in Makkah changed for the worse. The Prophet went to a town called Ta'if to call people to only worship Allah, thinking that he would find support there, but instead they set upon him. Young men and children started stoning him. He took shelter in a vineyard. A slave saw him there and gave him some grapes and water. After listening to the Prophet (peace be upon him) in the vineyard, he became a Muslim.

It is reported that the angel Gabriel came to him and asked his permission to punish the wrongdoers by bringing the mountains together and crushing them. The Prophet (peace be upon him) replied, "Allah has sent me as a mercy to mankind. Although these people may not believe, their children may."

Mi'raj – the Ascent to Heaven

It was at about this time that a miraculous event took place that gave the Prophet (peace be upon him) unbounded energy, and removed from his mind all the pain and shock of the deaths of Abu Talib and Khadijah, and of his suffering at Ta'if. What took place is central to Islam. It showed the Prophet and his Companions the highest reward and supreme pleasure that a human being can be given during his or her life on earth. This miraculous event was *al-mi'raj*. The Prophet was taken by Gabriel on an animal like a horse with wings, called the *buraq,* to Jerusalem, where he met some of the other earlier Prophets and acted as their *imam* (their leader in prayer).

The angel Gabriel then asked the Prophet (peace be upon him) to drink from one of the three glasses of drink that he had brought, one containing water, one containing milk, and the other containing wine. The Prophet chose the milk. The angel Gabriel praised his choice, and said that the Prophet's religion would remain the natural way of life *(deen al-fitrah)*, that is, the way of life that is natural to humanity.

The angel Gabriel then took him up through the seven heavens where he met most of the important Prophets, from Adam to Ibrahim, and including Musa and Isa, (peace be upon them all). Then Muhammad (peace be upon him) was taken beyond the seventh heaven to the Glory of God's Divine Presence, where even Gabriel was not permitted to go.

This ascent was only made possible by Allah. It shows how Muhammad (peace be upon him) had dedicated himself totally to Allah. That is why Allah granted him a nearness which even the angel Gabriel did not have. The journey was also extremely significant for Islam and all the Muslims, since it was during this journey that Allah told the Prophet that it was His Will that he and the Muslims should do the prayer five times a day. In this way they too could receive Allah's grace and enter a state of spiritual awareness.

This instruction from Allah to pray five times a day resulted in *salah* (the prayer) becoming the central pillar of Islam. Through *salah*, a human being can reach nearness to God. That is why the Prophet said, "*Salah* is ascent *(mi'raj)* for a faithful person."

The Two Covenants of 'Aqabah

In 620 CE, shortly before the *mi'raj* occurred, six leading members of the Khazraj tribe who came from a town called Yathrib, which lay to the north of Makkah, had become Muslim. The following year, five of these and seven other leading members came to Makkah for *hajj* (pilgrimage), and they entered into an agreement with Muhammad (peace be upon him). They agreed to obey none but Allah, and not to steal, nor to commit adultery, nor to kill children, nor to disobey him. This agreement was made at a place near Makkah known as 'Aqabah, and so it came to be known as the First Covenant of 'Aqabah.

The Prophet (peace be upon him) sent one of his Companions, Musa bin 'Umair, to Yathrib to teach them the Qur'an and give them religious instruction.

In 622 CE seventy-three men and two women came from Yathrib for *hajj*. The Prophet thought of making an agreement with them. They agreed to meet at 'Aqabah. The Prophet discussed this with his uncle Abbas who joined them at 'Aqabah. Here they held a secret meeting with the group whose members were mostly from the Khazraj tribe, and some from the Aws tribe. They pledged to help and protect Muhammad (peace be upon him). Then they asked, "Tell us O Prophet of Allah, what will be our reward if we remain true to our oath?" The Prophet said, "Paradise." Then one by one they took hold of his outstretched hand and promised to protect him. The Prophet had already promised never to leave them. This agreement became known as the Second Covenant of 'Aqabah.

After this, the Prophet Muhammad (peace be upon him) instructed the Muslims to migrate to Yathrib.

Hijrah: the Migration to Madina

The Prophet's suffering and patience had reached their maximum limits. About three months after the Second Covenant of 'Aqabah, Muhammad (peace be upon him) received an instruction from Allah to leave Makkah. The Prophet went to Yathrib – which was then given a new name in his honour, Madina al-Munawwara, which means 'the illuminated city'. This journey is known as the *Hijrah*, or migration. The year of the *Hijrah* became the first year in the Hijri calendar, which the Muslims use to measure their months and years. This is what happened:

The Makkan unbelievers had been plotting to kill the Prophet (peace be upon him) for some time. But on the very night that they decided to put their plan into action, the Prophet asked Ali to sleep in his place in his bed, and the Prophet and Abu Bakr quietly left Makkah without being seen.

When the unbelievers realised that they had been fooled, they went out in search of the Prophet and came right up to the cave in Mount

Thawr in which he and Abu Bakr were hiding. When Abu Bakr heard their steps he was afraid. He said, "O Prophet, here they are coming, and we two are alone!" "No," said the Prophet, "We have a third." "Who?" asked Abu Bakr. "Allah," he replied.

In the meantime a spider had spun a web across the mouth of the cave, and a bird had laid its eggs in a nest which it had made in a bush near the entrance. It looked as if no one could have entered the cave without breaking the web and frightening away the bird. When the unbelievers saw this they went elsewhere. Thus Allah saved them. After three nights the Prophet (peace be upon him) and Abu Bakr set out towards Madina with a guide.

Several people met them on their way and became Muslim. They went with them towards Madina. They stopped for a night in an old woman's house. She had no food. But she had a she-goat which was dry. The Prophet (peace be upon him) asked her to bring the goat to him. He put his hand on its udder. It immediately filled up with milk. They milked the goat and each one of them had some of that milk to drink. After they had left, the goat, with the Prophet's blessing, continued to give plenty of milk to that old lady.

After travelling for about two weeks, the Prophet (peace be upon him) and his group reached Quba where they stayed for a few days and built a mosque. This was the first mosque to be built in the history of Islam.

Then they proceeded on towards Madina.

In the meantime most of the people of the two tribes of Aws and Khazraj had become Muslim. People from a few other tribes also joined them to welcome Muhammad (peace be upon him) as he drew near to Madina. They all wanted a strong leader to support them against the powerful Jewish tribes. Dressed in full military dress, and with drums and music, they went to the outskirts of Madina to welcome him. Their poets had prepared a beautiful song of welcome in his honour. A large group of children were singing it as they danced along to welcome the Prophet.

When the Prophet (peace be upon him) first arrived in Madina, he allowed his camel, which was called Qaswa', to stop where it wanted. The camel stopped at the door of his relative by his mother's side, Abu

Ayub Ansari. The Prophet decided to stay there. Then he bought a plot of land near the house and constructed the mosque which is still known today as the Prophet's mosque (*al-Masjid an-Nabawi*) with the help of his Companions. The Prophet also built two thatched rooms by the side of the mosque, one for his wife Sawdah – who was a widow whom he had married in Makkah some time after Khadijah's death – and the other for 'A'ishah, a daughter of Abu Bakr, who was betrothed to him.

The Muslim Community of Madina

Immediately after his arrival in Madina, the Prophet Muhammad (peace and blessings of Allah be upon him) did two things which set the whole pattern for the future of Islam and the Muslims. The first was to establish a close link between those who had emigrated from Makkah (the *Muhajirun*) and the helpers of Madina (the *Ansar*). He arranged, with the wholehearted consent of the Madinan Muslims, that each one of them should take one of the emigrants from Makkah as his brother and share with him his property and his life. Many of the Makkan Muslims accepted this generous offer on the condition that they would take money only as a loan. The shelter which was given to the emigrants formed an important bond which laid the foundations of Muslim brotherhood, and set a noble example for Muslims of all ages. It also saved the new community from any potential rivalries, and set the standard for the future Muslim community *(ummah)*.

The other thing which the Prophet (peace be upon him) did was to bring together the Muslim tribes, the Jewish tribes, and even those who worshipped many gods, in order to persuade them to live together in peace. The Prophet dictated the terms of this agreement which is generally known as the Covenant of Madina, and which principally governed the relationship between the Muslims and the Jews.

The Jews were very powerful in Madina. They were traders, merchants and usurers, and they controlled the economic life of the pagan tribes. The Covenant of Madina amounted to an agreement with them to live together in peace, to protect each other if Madina was attacked, and to grant each other the freedom for each community to practise its own religion. Some of the terms of this Covenant were as follows:

- The Muslims and the Jews were to live together in peaceful harmony.

- Neither of the two parties was to interfere with the faith of the other.

- If a third party were to attack, each of the two parties would be bound to help one another in the event of war.

- If Madina itself was attacked, both parties were to join hands to defend it.

- Both parties were to regard Madina as a sacred place, and bloodshed was to be forbidden there.

- The Prophet Muhammad (peace be upon him) was to be the final judge in the event of any dispute.

Thus a Muslim Community which did not deny the rights of non-Muslim people became the ideal model for all Muslims. Allah was the sovereign and the law-giver, and the Prophet Muhammad (peace be upon him) was its leader and arbitrator, its guide and administrator. The Muslims had found a centre, a law-giver and a judge. Tribal laws were replaced by the basic principles of justice – irrespective of caste, creed or colour. The straightforward, honest behaviour of which Ja'far had spoken to the Abyssinian king in the past could now become the basis not only for individual personal improvement, but also for the legal principles and rules of society.

The new Muslim Community had to be organised, disciplined, integrated and protected from the schemes of its opponents. Because of these new needs, new revelations started coming to the Prophet Muhammad (peace be upon him). Whereas many of the earlier revelations had been about the Creator and His Creation, many of these later revelations contained practical guidance about how to behave and live in this world, and how to prepare for the next world. As the Prophet Muhammad himself said (peace be upon him):

"Live in this world as if you were going to live here for a thousand years, and prepare for the next world as if you were going to die tomorrow."

The New Direction for Prayers

During the second Hijri year, Muhammad (peace be upon him) received a revelation that the Muslims should face the Kaaʻba in Makkah whenever they prayed. Until then they had prayed facing towards the site of the Temple which had been built by the Prophet Solomon (peace be upon him) in Jerusalem, but which had been destroyed by the Romans several centuries earlier. Since the Kaaʻba had originally been built by the Prophet Adam for the worship of Allah, and had later been rebuilt by the Prophet Ibrahim (peace be upon them), this change in direction meant that the Muslims now identified themselves more closely with the pure ancient religious tradition of Adam and Eve, and of Ibrahim and Ismaʻil. The direction which Muslims face when they pray is known as the *qiblah*.

The Importance of Makkah

From this point on, Makkah started occupying a central place in the hearts of all new Muslims, and not just the emigrants who had left everything in Makkah to be with their beloved Prophet in Madina, (peace be upon him). The city of Makkah was to be treated from now on not just as the birth place of the Prophet, nor simply as the place having the house of Allah, but also as a meeting place for all Muslims. It had become the centre of Islam, the holiest of holy places, the holy sanctuary for all Muslims for all ages.

How the *Adhan* (the Call to Prayer) Started

As we have already seen, after the *mi'raj* (ascent) of Muhammad (peace be upon him), it became obligatory for all Muslims to pray five times a day. When they all came to Madina and their numbers increased, the Muslims needed to have a way of knowing when it was time to do each of the five prayers, so that they could all pray together.

One night a Companion of the Prophet met someone in a dream who taught him the call to prayer *(adhan)* which the Muslims still use today. He reported his dream to the Prophet (peace be upon him), who said, "It is a genuine vision," and told the Companion to teach the call to Bilal, the black slave who had once suffered such severe torture because he had accepted Islam before being freed by Abu Bakr. Thus the first call to prayer was given by Bilal. The person who gives this call to prayer is known as the *mu'adhdhin* (sometimes written as *muezzin*) and the call is known as the *adhan*. After the *adhan*, Muslims are asked to stand in rows behind the leader of the prayer *(imam)*, so that they can all pray together.

New Revelations for the Complete Way of Life

During the first three years after the *Hijrah*, the Prophet (peace be upon him) received many new revelations. These included commands to fast *(sawm)* during the month of *Ramadan,* to give money due to the poor *(zakah)*, and to prohibit the charging of interest in all transactions. Wine drinking and gambling were also prohibited. Laws regarding marriage and divorce, the rights of married women, inheritance and orphans were also revealed to the Prophet during this period.

All these revelations came as solutions for new situations. But although they came as solutions to particular problems, they were also designed to serve as general principles to be applied to all such occasions or similar situations. These principles, and all the other rules and regulations which were revealed to the Prophet Muhammad (peace be upon him) by Allah through the angel Gabriel, form what is known as the *Shari'ah*, the Divine Law for humanity, which still applies today.

Jihad Begins

The revelations in Makkah had told the Muslims to bear suffering with patience. In Madina, the order came for the Muslims to protect Islam because the Quraysh were now planning to attack the Muslims and to destroy them. The only way to establish peace now was by conquering

Makkah, the headquarters of the Quraysh tribe and the centre for the Muslims. Allah's message came in the very first Hijri year:

> Leave is given to those who fight because
> they were wronged – and surely Allah is able
> to help them. (*Qur'an*, 22: 39)

The Prophet Muhammad (peace be upon him) explained that this permission to fight had been granted only to preserve the Truth, and not in order to benefit oneself or one's party or one's country. And fighting was justified only when all other means of trying to establish peace had been exhausted. The Qur'an condemns bloodshed and war (for example, *Qur'an*, 6: 151, 17: 33, and 4: 93), but fighting in the way of Allah is obligatory if the opponents of Islam start destroying Allah's order. That is why this verse was revealed in Madina:

> And fight in the way of Allah against those
> who fight against you, but do not attack first:
> Allah does not love the aggressors. (*Qur'an*, 2: 190)

Even when the enemy wants to fight, the duty of Muslims is to invite them to peace. The Prophet (peace be upon him) told Mu'adh bin Jabal, the commander of the Muslim army:

> Do not fight them before you have called them (either to submit to Allah and accept Islam, or to make a peace treaty and pay tribute). And if they refuse, do not fight them until they take the initiative, and when they do, wait until they slay your men. Then, show them the bodies of the slain and say to them, "Is there no better way than this?" If Allah ordains that one single man from amongst them should submit to Him through your example, it will be better for you than to own the whole world. (Al-Bukhari)

Jihad means 'strife' or 'struggle', that is, using one's powers to the utmost in fighting against something which has earned God's disapproval.

Ultimately the purpose of *jihad* is self-purification and the purification of society. From the actions of the Prophet Muhammad (peace be upon him) and from the revelations of Allah, we learn that Muslims should be ready to defend the Truth and to fight when attacked.

The Battle of Badr

After the Muslims of Makkah had emigrated to Madina, the Makkans seized their property and went to Damascus to trade with this wealth. As it was Muslim property that was being used by the Quraysh to trade, the Prophet (peace be upon him) decided to intervene and capture their goods as they were returning, since their caravan would have to go past Madina.

When the Muslims heard that Abu Sufyan, a Quraysh leader of Makkah, was returning from Syria with a large caravan of goods, they decided to retrieve some of their losses. The Prophet gave the Muslims permission to attack and nearly all the Muslims prepared for this raid. Abu Sufyan guessed that the Muslims were nearby when date seeds from the dates of Madina were found in amongst the camel dung at Badr, a watering-place outside Madina, and so he sent a message to Makkah for help. Abu Jahl, the other principal leader of the Quraysh, came out in support with a fully armed contingent of more than a thousand men. Abu Sufyan himself took a different route and returned safely to Makkah. But the Prophet (peace be upon him) and the Muslims were confronted by Abu Jahl and his army at Badr.

The Muslims had only 313 men. But Allah granted them victory, helping them in the Unseen with an army of angels. Most of the leading people of Makkah, including Abu Jahl, were killed and a large group of Makkans were captured. Among the captured Makkans was Abbas, an uncle of the Prophet (peace be upon him). He and a few others accepted Islam but went back to Makkah. The rest had to be ransomed by the Makkans.

This decisive victory, apparently won by only a handful of Muslims, convinced many tribes that they were indeed being helped by Allah, and that Muhammad (peace be upon him) was indeed the Prophet and Messenger of Allah.

The Battle of Uhud

In retaliation for the defeat at Badr, the Quraysh prepared an army of 3,000 men and one year later they tried to enter Madina by force. This is why a battle took place on the mountain range of Uhud, which is just outside Madina, in the third Hijri year.

The Prophet placed a row of archers on the high ground behind the Muslim army as a defence, and instructed them never to leave their position. With their rear thus protected, the Muslims only had to deal with what was in front of them.

Khalid, who later became a great Muslim general, was at that time fighting on the side of the Quraysh. He planned a trick, feigning defeat and retreating so as to encourage the Muslims to advance and loot. The archers on the high ground were tempted by greed and, leaving their position, they joined in the chase. Khalid immediately brought his men around behind the Muslims and attacked them from behind, as they were now defenceless.

Even the Prophet (peace be upon him) was hurt, and one of his teeth was broken, but his closest Companions never left him. The Muslims managed to gather together again, and joined by others, they rallied successfully and a defeat was averted. Then, in the afternoon, they retreated to higher ground, regrouped properly, and were able to attack again.

The Makkans were not prepared to accept the high losses which they would have to suffer if they tried to attack once more, and so they decided to retreat. The Prophet (peace be upon him) sent a party of Muslims in pursuit to ensure that they did not return.

Many Muslims became martyrs during this battle, the most outstanding one being Hamzah, who was an uncle of the Prophet (peace be upon him).

After the battle, Allah sent down revelations warning all the Muslims that this had been a test from Allah, and that the losses which they had suffered had been because of their disobedience to the Prophet (peace be upon him) when they had greedily chased after booty. This was thus a severe lesson for future guidance. The following verses were revealed after the battle as a warning:

Allah was true to His promise towards you
when you made them flee by His leave – until
you lost heart, and disagreed about the order,
and disobeyed it, after He had shown you
what you desired.

Some of you there are that desire this world,
and some of you there are that desire the next world.

Then He made you flee from them, that He might try you;
and now He has pardoned you; and Allah is generous
to the believers. (*Qur'an*, 3: 152)

The Battle of Ahzab (the Battle of the Trench)

The outcome of the battle of Uhud had been indecisive and it encouraged the unbelievers of Makkah to attack again. In the fifth Hijri year, the Quraysh raised an army of 10,000 men and proceeded towards Madina.

The Quraysh army was supported by the Banu Nadir, one of the Jewish tribes which had been a party to the Covenant of Madina. This tribe had been expelled from Madina when it was discovered that they were plotting to kill the Prophet (peace be upon him), thus breaking the Covenant, and becoming an enemy.

The Banu Nadir had moved from Madina to Khaybar, a large Jewish settlement outside Madina, and joined the Makkan Quraysh, assuring them of the assistance of the other Jewish tribes which were still living in Madina.

On the advice of Salman al-Farsi, the only Persian Companion of the Prophet, a deep and wide trench was dug around the unprotected parts of Madina. The Prophet Muhammad (peace be upon him) himself helped to dig the trench. At one point his pickaxe hit an iron boulder and a flash of light seemed to spark out. He swung his pickaxe again and there was another spark and a flash. Yet again he swung his pickaxe and as the rock disintegrated there was another spark and a flash.

The Prophet (peace be upon him) said that in these three flashes of light he was shown how first the Arabian peninsula, and then the Roman Empire, and then the Persian Empire, would be defeated and conquered by the Muslims. He told his Companions of this to give them strength and assure them of victory.

When they arrived at the outskirts of Madina, the army of the Quraysh was surprised by the deep and wide trench which confronted them. They had never seen anything like it before. They laid siege. In the meantime they made contact with the Banu Qurayzah, another Jewish tribe of Madina which, like the Banu Nadir, intended to betray the Muslims. The Prophet (peace be upon him) sent them a warning but they did not repent, nor did they stop their treacherous planning to help the Quraysh and attack the Muslims from behind. Thanks to a man called Nu'aym, however, who had once been an ally of the Quraysh, their plans were foiled.

Unknown to the Quraysh and the Banu Qurayzah, Nu'aym had recognised the truth and become a Muslim. First he visited the leaders of the Banu Qurayzah, and then he visited the leaders of the army of the Quraysh, awakening in each the fear that the other would not help if the Muslims started winning. As a result, both the Quraysh and the Banu Qurayzah were unwilling to trust each other and did nothing for several days. Their food began to run out and they began to lose confidence. Then the weather changed. Stormy winds, thunder and rain blew away the tents of the enemy, and made it impossible for them to cook what little food was left. In the end they had to retreat in dismay and disorder in the middle of the night. When the Muslims saw that the army of the Quraysh had run away, they knew that Allah had helped them yet again.

After the war was over, the Banu Qurayzah were asked to choose someone to judge them for their secret betrayal and breach of the Covenant of Madina at a moment of crisis. They chose Sa'd, the chief of Aws, a tribe which had always been friendly to them in the past. According to Sa'd's judgement, which was in accordance with the penalty for treachery which is contained in the Torah, all male adults who refused to accept Islam were beheaded and the rest had to leave Madina.

The Treaty of Hudaibiyah

In the sixth Hijri year, the Prophet Muhammad (peace be upon him) had a dream that he was visiting the Kaa'ba and walking round it. He decided to act according to his dream and to visit the Kaa'ba. With him went 1400 of his followers. When the Quraysh learnt about this venture, they decided to stop the Prophet and his followers from entering Makkah. The Prophet and his followers were not fully armed – they had just their swords for personal protection. After intensive negotiations with the Prophet (peace be upon him), the Quraysh leaders signed a treaty with him. As the Muslims had been waiting at a place outside Makkah which was called Hudaibiyah, this treaty came to be known as the Treaty of Hudaibiyah. One of the things which the representative of the Quraysh said was this:

> O people, I have been sent as an envoy to kings – to Caesar and to Chosroes and to the Negus – and I have not seen any king whose men so honour him as the companions of Muhammad honour Muhammad. If he commands anything, they rush to fulfil it; when he does *wudu*, they almost fight for the water that he has used; when he speaks, their voices are hushed in his presence; and they will not look at him full in the face, but lower their eyes out of respect for him. He has offered you good terms, so accept them from him.

The terms of the Treaty were briefly as follows:

1. For the next ten years people were to enjoy peace and refrain from fighting each other.

2. There would be security of person and property for the Prophet's Companions if they travelled to Makkah for *hajj* or *'umrah*, the greater and the lesser pilgrimages, or for commerce on their way to Yemen or Ta'if – and the same security for the Quraysh if they went to Madina on their way to Syria or Iraq for trade or commerce.

3.	Anyone from Makkah who joined the Prophet without the permission of the Quraysh would be handed back to the Quraysh, but anyone who left Madina to join the Quraysh in Makkah would not be handed back to the Prophet.

4.	Anyone who wanted could become an ally either of the Prophet or of the Quraysh.

5.	There was to be no violation of the treaty and no treachery.

6.	The Prophet and the Muslims were to return to Madina that year, without visiting the Kaaʿba as they had intended, although their sacrificial animals could be sacrificed outside the precincts of Makkah.

7.	The following year the Prophet and his Companions would be allowed to enter Makkah and stay there for three nights, during which time the Quraysh would keep out of sight.

Most of the Companions did not fully understand the implications of the Treaty, but the Prophet (peace be upon him) insisted that everything had been done under Allah's direction. That was why Allah had sent down a revelation saying, "Surely We have given you a manifest victory." (Qur'an, 48: 1).

Although the third clause of the treaty seemed to be rather humiliating for the Muslims, it ultimately proved beneficial for them. Because of this clause, the Prophet (peace be upon him) had to send one man back to the Quraysh, but he managed to kill his captors and returned to the Prophet in Madina. The Prophet insisted on honouring the Treaty, however, and still would not allow him to stay. Accordingly this man joined up with several other new Muslims who were in a similar position and who could not join the Prophet in Madina, and they based themselves outside Makkah, attacking Makkan caravans and carrying on guerrilla warfare against the Quraysh. As a result, it was the Makkan Quraysh themselves who finally requested the Prophet (peace be upon him) to drop Clause 3 from the Treaty.

The fourth and fifth clauses of the Treaty were eventually violated, by some allies of the Quraysh: Two years after the Treaty had been signed, the Banu Bakr tribe (who were allies of the Quraysh) attacked the Banu Khuza'ah tribe (who were allies of the Prophet) while they were asleep. When the allies of the Prophet (peace be upon him) took refuge near the Kaa'ba they were butchered in its sacred precincts. The Prophet immediately declared that the Treaty of Hudaibiyah was no longer binding. During the two years of peace which had lasted after the Treaty of Hudaibiyah, three important things happened:

- The Banu Nadir, who had been expelled from Madina after plotting to kill the Prophet (peace be upon him) were attacked by the Prophet within two weeks of the signing of the Treaty of Hudaibiyah. The Prophet carried out the attack before they had time to declare themselves allies of the Quraysh, and therefore immune from attack under the terms of the treaty. The Quraysh could not therefore come to the aid of the Banu Nadir tribe. The Banu Nadir were at this time living in the fortress of Khaybar, which was conquered by the Muslims after a hard struggle. Thus a vital centre for the enemies of Islam and the Muslims was destroyed.

- Two important members of the Makkan Quraysh, Khalid bin Walid, a great military genius who had been an invaluable asset to the Quraysh, and Amr Ibn al-'As, another Quraysh leader, embraced Islam.

- The Prophet (peace be upon him) sent letters to the Roman emperor, the Persian emperor, the ruler of Egypt, the king of Abyssinia, the chiefs of Syria and various other leaders inviting all of them to accept Islam. Only the king of Abyssinia accepted that he was the Messenger of Allah. Later, both the Roman emperor and the Persian emperor attacked Arabia in an attempt to destroy Islam and the Muslims – but without success. This happened during the last days of the Prophet (peace be upon him).

The Conquest of Makkah (630 CE)

Once the Quraysh had violated the Treaty of Hudaibiyah, the Treaty was now no longer binding. The Prophet (peace be upon him) secretly planned an invasion of Makkah. He marched with an army of 10,000 Muslims. When this army reached the outskirts of Makkah, the Quraysh realised that they would not be able to resist this force. Abu Sufyan secretly met the Prophet and accepted Islam. The Prophet then declared that whoever took shelter at Abu Sufyan's house would be safe from attack. As a result there was hardly any bloodshed. Only 11 people were killed.

After the Muslims' victorious entry into Makkah, the first thing the Prophet did (peace be upon him) was to destroy all the idols and cleanse the house of Allah. As the Prophet was clearing the Kaa'ba of all the idols, he recited the Qur'anic verse:

> We hurl the truth against falsehood
> and it prevails over it,
> and so it vanishes away." (*Qur'an*, 21: 18)

After removing the idols, the Prophet asked Bilal, the slave who had become the *mu'adhdhin* (the person who calls the Muslims to prayer), to give the *adhan* (the call to prayer), and the Prophet (peace be upon him) then led the prayer.

After the prayer, the Prophet called all the people of the Quraysh to come near the Kaa'ba and asked them, "What treatment do you expect from me?" They replied, "You are a noble brother to the young and a gentle nephew to the aged."

And the Prophet (peace be upon him) said, "I will treat you as Yusuf (Joseph) treated his brothers. You are free from all fear today. May Allah forgive you."

When the Makkans heard this, they could not believe it. Then, when they realised that he meant what he said, they were overwhelmed with joy and gratitude. Within a short while they rushed to accept Islam. The Prophet then addressed them and said:

There is no god but Allah. He is One and has no partner. He has fulfilled His promise and helped His servant and all by Himself He has crushed all the hosts. Today all false prides and silly customs are trampled down under my feet. You are the children of Adam – and Adam was created from dust. Allah says: "O people! We have created you from a male and a female, and We have divided you into tribes and families so that you may know one another. Surely the noblest amongst you in the sight of Allah is the most God-fearing amongst you. Surely Allah is Knowing, Aware." (*Qur'an*, 49: 13) ... Today Allah has forbidden the sale of wine (and all other intoxicants), and usury. (Ibn Ishaq, *The Life of Muhammad*).

The Prophet (peace be upon him) asked the Muslims who had emigrated from Makkah to Madina not to reclaim any of the property which they had left in Makkah, now that they were back. He entrusted the key of the Kaa'ba to 'Uthman bin Talha, who had once refused the Prophet entrance into the Kaa'ba in the days before the emigration to Madina and who had ill-treated him. The Prophet (peace be upon him) said, "If anyone takes the key of the Kaa'ba from 'Uthman bin Talha or his descendants he will be cruel." That is why the key is still with the same family to this day.

Eventually the other towns and tribes of the region followed the lead of Makkah and although there was still some resistance to the Prophet (peace be upon him), after the battle of Hunayn which was won by the Muslims, the whole of Arabia accepted Islam and became Muslim.

The Farewell Pilgrimage

After the conquest of Makkah, the Prophet Muhammad (peace be upon him) returned to Madina. He stayed there for a year and then, having led an expedition to Tabuk in northern Arabia in order to prevent a threatened invasion by the Roman army, in 10 AH (632 CE), he set out on his last and only pilgrimage *(hajj)*. In performing this pilgrimage, the Prophet (peace be upon him) not only fulfilled his duty to his Lord, but also taught everyone how to do the *hajj*. His example is still followed by the Muslims today. During one of the most important parts of the pilgrimage, when all the pilgrims were assembled on the plain of Arafat, the Prophet (peace be upon him) delivered his farewell speech in front of 120,000 pilgrims. After praising and thanking Allah, he said:

O people, listen carefully to what I say because I do not know whether I will meet you again on such an occasion. So listen to what I am saying to you very carefully and convey these words to those who could not be present here today.

O people, regard the life and property of each Muslim as a sacred trust, just as you regard this month, and this day and this city, as sacred. Remember that you will have to appear before Allah and give an account of all your actions. So do not stray from the straight path after I am gone. Return the things which have been kept by you as a trust (amanah) to their rightful owners.

All interest dues should be cancelled, and you must give back only the capital which you owe. Allah has forbidden interest (riba) – and I hereby cancel the interest dues payable to my uncle Abbas bin Abdul Muttalib.

O people, your wives have certain rights over you and you have certain rights over them. If they abide by your right over them, then to them belongs the right to be fed and clothed in kindness. Treat them well and be kind to them, for they are your partners and committed helpers. And it is your right that they do not make friends with anyone of whom you do not approve, and that they never commit adultery.

Beware of Satan, he is desperate in his attempts to divert you from the worship of Allah; so in following your religion, beware of him. He has lost all hope that he will ever be able to lead you astray in big things, so beware of following him in small things.

O people, listen with care. All believers are brothers. You are not allowed to take anything belonging to another Muslim unless he gives it to you willingly.

O people, no one is superior to another unless it be in that person's obedience to Allah. No Arab is superior to a non-Arab, unless it be in piety.

O people, reflect on what I am saying. I leave behind me two things – the Qur'an, and my Sunnah. If you follow them you will never go wrong.

Listen to me carefully. Worship Allah, do *salah* (prayer), observe *sawm* (fasting) during the month of *Ramadan*, and pay *zakah* (money which is due to the poor). Do the *hajj* (pilgrimage) if you can afford it.

O people, be mindful of those who work under you. Feed and clothe them as you feed and clothe yourselves.

O people, no prophet *(nabi)* or Messenger *(rasul)* will come after me and no new faith will come. All those who are listening to me should pass on my words to others and they to others again. It may be that the last ones will understand my words better than those who listen to me directly.

Have I conveyed the Message of Allah to you, O people?

The assembled pilgrims answered, "By Allah, you have." The Prophet (peace be upon him) raised his forefinger and said, "O Allah, bear witness!" As he finished speaking, the final revelation, which was the last verse of the Qur'an to be revealed, came to him:

Today I have perfected your way of life (*deen*) for you
and I have completed My blessings upon you,
and I have confirmed Islam as your religion. (*Qur'an*, 5: 3)

The Prophet's Last Days on Earth

After returning to Madina, the Prophet Muhammad (peace be upon him) fell ill. He became so ill that he could not lead the prayer or even, later, go to the mosque. At his command Abu Bakr started leading the prayer. One day the Prophet said that Allah had given him the choice of staying in the world or returning to Him, and that he had chosen to return. His only surviving daughter, Fatimah, was almost overwhelmed with sorrow when she heard her father's decision. The Prophet (peace be upon him) comforted her by whispering that she would be the first of his relations to join him in Paradise.

When his death was announced in the mosque, 'Umar could not believe it. He thought that the Prophet must be temporarily asleep and that people were trying to create mischief, so he brought out his sword and threatened to kill anyone who said that the Prophet had died. Abu Bakr went to the Prophet's house and saw that he had indeed died. He returned to the mosque, looked at 'Umar, and then addressed the crowd with tears in his eyes: "Surely he who worships Muhammad should know that Muhammad is dead, but he who worships Allah should know that Allah is alive and never dies." Then he recited the following verse of the Qur'an:

> Muhammad is only a Messenger;
> Messengers have passed away before him.
> Why, if he should die or is slain,
> will you turn back on your heels?
> If anyone should turn back on his heels,
> he will not harm Allah in any way;
> and Allah will reward the thankful. (*Qur'an*, 3: 144)

When he heard these words, 'Umar suddenly realised the truth of the Prophet's passing and he collapsed. At the same time, the Muslims felt reassured that Allah had not deserted them, even though their beloved Prophet had left the world, may the blessings and peace of Allah be on him, and on his family, and on his companions, and on all who follow him with sincerity, until the Last Day.

The Prophet's Final Achievement

As we noted earlier, a Prophet is a person chosen by Allah through whom Allah tells mankind about how to live and let others live in this world; about what is harmful for human beings and what is good for them; about what the relationship is between Allah, human beings and their environment; and about how men and women should organise their lives so as to avoid mishaps and disaster and become the true representatives of Allah on earth. The Prophet Muhammad (peace be upon him) did all of this.

The Prophet (peace be upon him) achieved all of this by means of the revelations which he received from Allah, by the example which he gave through his own character and behaviour, and, above all, by the transformation of character which his example brought about in his followers.

The Prophet (peace be upon him) thus left for human beings a supreme example of what the role of faith in Allah is in human life as a whole. And his life embodied all the basic features of Islam:

- Islam demands complete self-surrender to God, including a readiness to be patient and the ability to accept suffering.

- Islam is a complete way of life and provides the means to establish conditions in which such a way of life can be practised. This assurance was granted by Allah to the Prophet (peace be upon him) during his time in Makkah. And the establishment of the Muslim Community of Madina did not mean that it was necessary to change his approach — it was a necessary consequence of the command to establish the *deen* of Allah on earth. The emigration from Makkah to Madina (the *Hijrah*) was not a 'flight', but a planned withdrawal with the intention of setting up a Muslim community in a place where Islam could be practised freely, and where the message which reveals the Truth of Allah could prevail over the hostility of unbelievers misguided by falsehood.

- The "manifest victory" which occurred again and again in the Prophet's life (peace be upon him) is a clear indication of Allah's presence, guidance and help.

- *Jihad,* or fighting in the way of Allah, is an appropriate way of establishing the Truth. Muslims should be ready to sacrifice their lives and their property in the way of Allah.

- Death is not a tragedy. It is only a doorway, which leads from the life of this world through to the life of the next world. To die in the way of Allah is to gain the status of a martyr – and whoever becomes a martyr goes straight to Paradise – but one must not fight simply in order to become a martyr, but rather in order to gain victory in the way of Allah.

- Love for the Truth is more important than anything else. This is shown by having love of Allah and His Messenger, Muhammad, may the peace and blessings of Allah be on him. Thus *Jihad* is both a test and a demonstration of a Muslim's love for Truth – in other words, of that person's *iman* (faith).

The Prophet's Personality

The Qur'an Personified

When some young people requested the Prophet's wife 'A'ishah to say something about the character of the Prophet (peace be upon him) she asked, "Haven't you read the Qur'an?"

They replied, "Yes."

"He is the Qur'an personified," she said.

By that she meant that whatever the Qur'an says about morality, virtue, spiritual nearness to God and knowledge, was to be found in the Prophet. He (peace be upon him) embodied the message which he brought.

A Mercy to the Entire Creation

The Qur'an says that Muhammad (peace be upon him) is declared by Allah to be a Mercy from Allah to the entire creation (*Qur'an*, 21: 107). Kindness was thus the most outstanding characteristic of his nature.

A Perfect Man

The Qur'an also says that Muhammad (peace be upon him) was a man with tremendous moral perfection (*Qur'an*, 68: 4). It has been reported by Jabir, a Companion, that the Prophet (peace be upon him) said, "Allah sent me to perfect good qualities and to complete good deeds." It is by reflecting on the Prophet Muhammad's actions that we can see the example of a perfect human being.

How the Prophet Attained to this State of Perfection

What the Prophet Muhammad (peace be upon him) told Ali makes it easy for us to understand why he was such a perfect human being. His way of living and behaviour were summed up by him in the following statement:

> • Abstinence is my avocation • Agony is my attendant • Brotherly love is my method • Confidence is my asset • Faith is my strength • *Jihad* is my career • Knowledge is my weapon • Patience is my dress • Pleasure of Allah is my prize • Intellect is the basis of my religion • Remembrance of Allah is my delight • Revelation is my capital • Submission is my protection • Truth is my support • Zeal is my horse • The light of my eye is *salah* (prayer) • (Hadith)

The Prophet Muhammad (peace be upon him) set the example of how to submit wholeheartedly to Allah, of how to be truthful and never to tell a lie even jokingly, of how to be kind not only to human beings but also to animals and plants, of how to be forgiving and generous even to those who are enemies. He used to say, "Allah will not show mercy to the person who does not show mercy to others."

The Prophet Muhammad (peace be upon him) would never call a slave "slave". He advised his Companions to address a slave as "my son" or "my daughter", and he also told them to, "Forgive them 70 times a day." Not only did he free Zaid, he advised his Companions to free their slave girls and then to marry them, and never to use them as concubines.

He appreciated the high status of women and recognised how much depends on the way a mother raises her young: "Paradise lies at the feet of the mother." And at the same time he recognised the noble status of men whose duty it is to fight for the Truth: "Paradise lies under the shadow of the sword."

The Prophet Muhammad (peace be upon him) was an orphan. He was always kind to orphans. He said, "If anyone pats an orphan's head, and does so only for Allah's sake, then he will have blessings for every hair over which his hand has passed, and as for anyone who treats well an orphan girl or boy under his care, he and I shall be very close."

The Prophet Muhammad (peace be upon him) was also very kind to the poor. He used to pray, "O Allah keep me alive as a poor man, and make me die as a poor man, and bring me back to life in the company of the poor."

Whenever the Prophet received, after a *jihad*, one fifth of the spoils of war, he would distribute everything among the poor, and would not keep a single thing for the next day. He could not sleep at night if there was any money in his possession. His generosity was boundless. He would even pay off the debts of people who had died. He never said "No" to anyone who asked for his help. His courtesy was proverbial, and he was always the first to greet other people. He always showed respect to elders. Whenever his foster mother Halimah came to visit him he would get up and spread his cloak for her to sit on.

The Prophet Muhammad (peace be upon him) was thus the most perfect human representative of Allah on the earth – *khalifatullah*. Whenever we try to find an example of any kind of human goodness, we find in him the greatest example of that quality. He is, as Allah Himself has said, the most perfect ideal for all humanity – *uswatun hasanah*.